A BLOODY WEEK

To the Arnhem Irish, both native-born and of Irish descent, whose involvement in Operation Market Garden (17–26 September 1944), the largest airborne operation in history, must be acknowledged and never forgotten, and that for which they fought must not be lost.

Lieutenant Colonel Dan Harvey, now retired, served on operations at home and abroad for forty years, including tours of duty in the Middle East, Africa, the Balkans and South Caucasus, with the UN, EU, NATO PfP and OSCE. He is the author of *A Bloody Dawn: The Irish At D-Day* (2019); *Soldiering against Subversion: The Irish Defence Forces and Internal Security During the Troubles, 1969–1998* (2018); *Into Action: Irish Peacekeepers Under Fire, 1960–2014* (2017); *A Bloody Day: The Irish at Waterloo* and *A Bloody Night: The Irish at Rorke's Drift* (both reissued 2017); and *Soldiers of the Short Grass: A History of the Curragh Camp* (2016).

IN THIS SERIES

A Bloody Day: The Irish at Waterloo (2017)

A Bloody Night: The Irish at Rorke's Drift (2017)

A Bloody Dawn: The Irish at D-Day (2019)

A BLOODY WEEK

THE IRISH AT ARNHEM

DAN HARVEY

MERRION
PRESS

First published in 2019 by
Merrion Press
An imprint of Irish Academic Press
10 George's Street
Newbridge
Co. Kildare
Ireland
www.merrionpress.ie

9781785372735 (Paper)
9781785372742 (Kindle)
9781785372759 (Epub)
9781785372766 (PDF)

British Library Cataloguing in Publication Data
An entry can be found on request

Library of Congress Cataloging in Publication Data
An entry can be found on request

Typeset in Bembo MT Std 11/15 pt

Cover front: The Allied campaign in North-West Europe, June 1944–May 1945: the British Airborne Division at Arnhem and Oosterbeek in Holland © Imperial War Museum.
Cover back: INTERFOTO/Alamy Stock Photo.

CONTENTS

Maps   vii

Acknowledgements   xi

Preface   xii

Introduction   1

1. Montgomery's Audacious Plan   5

2. Bound for Holland   18

3. The Operation Gets Underway (17 September 1944)   26

4. Trapped in Arnhem (18 September 1944)   40

5. The Enemy Regroups (19 September 1944)   49

6. Inside the Perimeter (20 September 1944)   56

7. Der Hexenkessel (The Witches' Cauldron)
(21 September 1944)   63

8. Black Friday (22 September 1944)   69

9. Under Bombardment (23 September 1944)   77

10. Against All Odds (24 September 1944)   85

11. Operation Berlin (25–26 September 1944)   95

12. Telling the Story of Operation Market Garden   103

Epilogue   110

Bibliography   119

Glossary   120

Abbreviations   123

Chronology   124

Index   131

Operation Market Garden

1ST BRITISH AIRBOURNE DIVISION

Arnhem

Driel

Waal

Nijmegen

Rhine

82ND U.S. AIRBOURNE DIVISION

Maas

Cleve

Grave

Reichswald

's-Hertogenbosh

GERMANY

NETHERLANDS

GERMAN ATTACKS 21–25 SEPT.

Tilburg

GERMAN ATTACKS 21–25 SEPT.

101ST U.S. AIRBOURNE DIVISION

Wilhelmina Canal

26TH SEPT.

Helmond

Eindhoven

FRONT LINE LAST LIGHT – 26TH SEPT.

12TH CORPS

30TH CORPS

30TH CORPS

8TH CORPS

FRONT LINE LAST LIGHT – 26TH SEPT.

Venlo

Maas

NETHERLANDS

FRONT LINE NOON – 17TH SEPT.

BELGIUM

N

Arnhem Bridge and Oosterbeek Permimeter

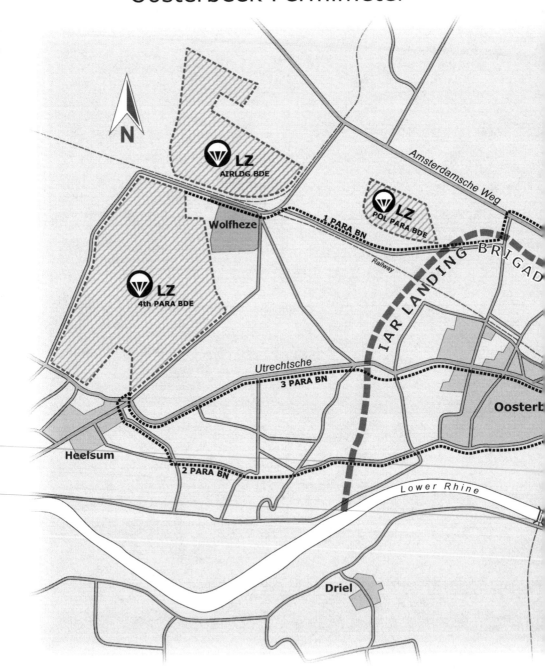

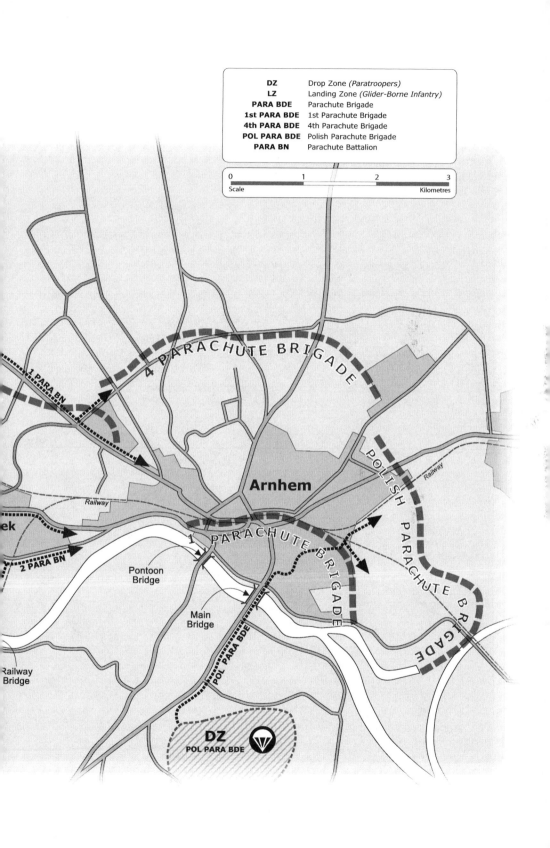

DZ	Drop Zone *(Paratroopers)*
LZ	Landing Zone *(Glider-Borne Infantry)*
PARA BDE	Parachute Brigade
1st PARA BDE	1st Parachute Brigade
4th PARA BDE	4th Parachute Brigade
POL PARA BDE	Polish Parachute Brigade
PARA BN	Parachute Battalion

0   1   2   3
Scale   Kilometres

4 PARACHUTE BRIGADE

1 PARA BN

POLISH PARACHUTE BRIGADE

Arnhem

Railway

Railway

ek

2 PARA BN

1 PARACHUTE BRIGADE

Pontoon Bridge

Main Bridge

POL PARA BDE

Railway Bridge

DZ
POL PARA BDE

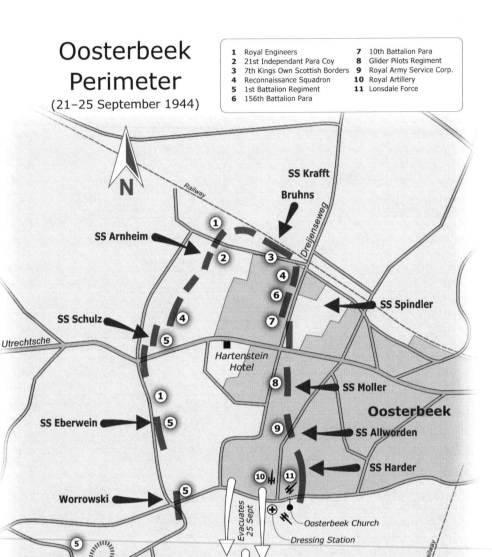

Oosterbeek Perimeter

(21–25 September 1944)

1	Royal Engineers	**7**	10th Battalion Para
2	21st Independant Para Coy	**8**	Glider Pilots Regiment
3	7th Kings Own Scottish Borders	**9**	Royal Army Service Corp.
4	Reconnaissance Squadron	**10**	Royal Artillery
5	1st Battalion Regiment	**11**	Lonsdale Force
6	156th Battalion Para		

N

Railway

SS Krafft

Bruhns

Dreijenseweg

SS Arnheim

SS Spindler

SS Schulz

Utrechtsche

Hartenstein Hotel

SS Moller

Oosterbeek

SS Eberwein

SS Allworden

SS Harder

Worrowski

Evacuates 25 Sept

Oosterbeek Church

Dressing Station

Westerbouwing

Hevedorp Ferry

Lower Rhine

Railway

Scale 0   0.5   1   2 Kilometres

Driel

ACKNOWLEDGEMENTS

Death is always a difficult and distressing experience, but there is a sense of added sadness and loneliness when someone dies far away from home and loved ones. In wartime this tragedy is compounded when the victim of hostilities has no known grave. After the Second World War, great efforts were made to recover, identify and reinter the remains of the dead in Commonwealth War plots. Unfortunately, it was not always possible to find the bodies in order to retrieve them; perhaps the section of the battlefield on which they fell was subject to aerial bombing, artillery barrage or fire and building collapse, leaving families and loved ones wondering and the army helpless, unable to reassure them, the soldier's passing somehow lacking finality and remaining a cause of upset beyond grief – a kind of suspended isolation.

Not for these families the comfort of a named cemetery and precise references of plot, row and grave number, and of course an individual headstone. Yet, memorials, monuments, statues and other objects – commemorations, customs and remembrances – all salute, honour and pay tribute to the wartime dead, marking their contribution and sacrifice. The occasioning of anniversaries in particular give a precise focus to our recollection of their dedication, determination, deeds and the manner of their death. To remember them evokes bittersweet emotions of both pride and pathos. Beyond the sadness, however, we value, respect and hold dear the worth of their contribution, effort and sacrifice.

In writing this book, I wish to thank the generosity of spirit of David Truesdale, whose original research he so graciously and willingly shared and

Acknowledgements

whose 2002 book, *Brotherhood of the Cauldron: Irishmen with the 1st Airborne Division from North Africa to Arnhem*, is an important telling of the story of the Irish in Operation Market Garden. I also wish to thank Richard Doherty, whose encouragement was hugely significant, both in the early stages and throughout the writing of this book. To Conor Graham, Fiona Dunne, Keith Devereux and Maeve Convery at Irish Academic Press/Merrion Press. To Deirdre Maxwell, for the typing of the handwritten manuscript, and Paul O'Flynn, for his technical assistance, I wish to express my sincere and heartfelt thanks.

PREFACE

Coming in over Arnhem in his stricken Dakota aircraft, Cork-born David 'Lummy' Lord wondered how much longer he could keep the plane in the air. His C-47 Dakota was one of a number of Douglas aircraft of 271 Squadron, 46 Group RAF that had been hit by German ground fire, and Lord's plane was forced to descend to about 500 feet, the starboard wing ablaze. An experienced pilot, Lord was able to maintain lift and keep the nose of the Dakota above the artificial horizon on his instrument panel, thus sustaining level flight. However, he and his crew were all too aware this could cease to be the case at any second, the wing might crumple under pressure and suddenly collapse, and with its disintegration flight would be impossible and they would immediately fall to earth.

Born in Cork in 1913, his father was a warrant officer in the Royal Welsh Fusiliers posted to Ireland who had married Mary Ellen, a local Cork girl. Their son, David Samuel Anthony Lord, had joined the RAF in August 1936 as an airman, rising quickly through the ranks. On becoming a Sergeant Pilot he was sent to India, and commissioned as pilot officer in May 1942 he flew over Burma in support of Operation Longcloth, Orde Wingate's first Chindit expedition. During his time there he was awarded an Air Officer Commanding's Commendation and a Mention in Dispatches (MID) receiving a Distinguished Flying Cross (DFC) in July 1943. By January 1944 he had returned to the UK for service with 271 Squadron based at RAF Down Ampney, Gloucestershire, where he trained to drop paratroopers, supplies and to tow military gliders. Six months later, on the night of 5–6 June as part of Operation Overlord, he had dropped British airborne soldiers over Normandy to secure the flanks of the seaborne invaders on D-Day, the beginning of the great campaign to open the 'Second Front' in the liberation of Europe, to restore freedom from Nazi fascism and make the world safe once again. Flying then as now through intense anti-aircraft fire, his Dakota was left with a hole in the rudder and damage to its elevator and hydraulics system. Over the next few weeks, he flew a series of missions to drop supplies to the Allied troops in the expanding Normandy beachhead.

Operation Market Garden (17–26 September 1944) was one of the most audacious and controversial operations of the Second World War. A simultaneous two-part synchronised airborne drop (the 'Market' part of the operation) with a coincident armoured column ground advance (the 'Garden' part), the aim of the mission was to secure and hold a number of vital bridges along a 64-mile 'corridor' into German-occupied Holland. Together, they would punch a hole in the German defences and spectacularly seize a 'start line' location for the next phase of operations, the advance into the Ruhr, the industrial heartland of Germany, with the overall intended aim of ending the war in Europe before the close of 1944. The stakes were high and the mood was optimistic, but German resistance had been greater than expected and the fighting became protracted. Resupply was now vital.

Taking off from Down Ampney Airfield on 19 September 1944, Flight Lieutenant David Samuel Anthony 'Lummy' Lord's objective was to reach Supply Dropping Zone 'Victor' just north of Oosterbeek, a village about 5 km (3.1 miles) west of Arnhem in the Netherlands on a resupply mission. During the battle for Arnhem Bridge, the Royal Air Force (RAF) and the United States Army Air Force (USAAF) played a major role in both 'dropping' the British 1st Airborne Division into the Arnhem area, and flying in reinforcements and supplies once the battle had got underway to the now beleaguered troops. The struggle for control of the Dutch town was in its third day, the German opposition had been underestimated and the fighting was fierce.

Two days earlier, on 17 September, he had been part of the initial airlift to Arnhem, returning the following day again towing a Horsa troop-carrying glider for the second airlift when he experienced anti-aircraft fire and his Dakota was damaged by flak. Nonetheless, he delivered the Horsa he was towing safely over its landing zone and returned back to England. Now on his third run over Arnhem on a desperately needed ammunition resupply air mission, his Dakota's starboard wing was hit by anti-aircraft ground fire. Despite being fully justified to break off his mission and return to base, instead he continued. With the starboard wing on fire, he determinedly reduced height to 900 feet to ensure accuracy of the drop, where his aircraft was singled out for the concentrated fire of the anti-aircraft guns below. Climbing again after the run, and with the thought of attempting the flight back to England beginning to form in his mind, he was informed by his crew that there were still two panniers of ammunition remaining. His reaction was not to head for safety, but rather to go back for a second approach and ensure the ground troops received the ammunition he knew they needed. To the admiration of those on the ground who witnessed the unfolding episode and despite his obvious difficulties, he descended to 500 feet and successfully dropped the remaining supply of ammunition to its designated drop zone. That achieved, he was now struggling to gain height and maintain level flight in order for the crew to bail out in a safe and organised manner. However, the damaged starboard wing collapsed, suddenly giving way and folding back on itself. The aircraft sharply foundered, went into a decisive and destructive swirling nosedive and plummeted into a ploughed field below.

Thrown clear, the only survivor was the navigator, Flight Lieutenant Harry King, who was captured by German forces and spent the rest of the war as a prisoner. The remainder of the crew all perished. The sacrifice of David Lord was made manifestly more moving because the supplies that he and his crew died to deliver fell directly into enemy hands; the German army had overrun the supply drop zones and malfunctioning British signal corps radio communications had been unable to inform the RAF. It was only on the release of Flight Lieutenant King in 1945 that the full story became known, and for his actions Flight Lieutenant David 'Lummy' Lord was awarded a posthumous Victoria Cross.

INTRODUCTION

After D-Day, with the collapse of German resistance in France and Belgium, by late August 1944 the end of the war was within sight and Operation Market Garden was designed to bring it within reach. The Operation was imaginative, daring and simple, and nothing like it had ever been attempted before. It was the first time airborne troops were to be used strategically by the Allies on such a scale; 35,000 of them were to be flown a distance of 300 miles from England and dropped behind enemy lines to seize and hold a series of bridges in Holland. The aim was to allow an Allied armoured column of Corps strength to advance sixty-four miles into enemy-held territory in order to consolidate a bridgehead, from which the Allies could further their offensive. Surprise and speed were crucial to the success of Operation Market Garden, the prize being a secure start line to strike into Germany itself.

Selected to deliver the surprise element, the 'Market' part of the operation was the newly-formed First Allied Airborne Army commanded by a United States Army Air Force officer, Lieutenant General Lewis Hyde Brereton. His second-in-command was British Lieutenant General Frederick Arthur Montague 'Boy' Browning. The First Allied Airborne Army consisted of US and British paratrooper divisions and US and British infantry glider-borne brigades (the specific brigades making up the First Allied Airborne Army were the US 82nd and 101st Airborne Divisions whilst the British divisions were the 1st and 6th Airborne and also the 1st Special Air Service Brigade and Polish 1st Independent Parachute Brigade). These paratrooper and infantry glider-borne divisions were dependent on the

Royal Air Force (RAF) and United States Army Air Force (USAAF) to transport them into battle, so General Brereton's command also included the 38 and 46 Groups RAF, 9th US Troop Carrier Command USAAF and the Glider Pilot Regiment.

The British 6th Airborne Division had only just returned from the campaign in Normandy and the advance to the Seine, a three-month period during which it was in almost daily 'contact' with the enemy, and it was resting and recuperating. The US 82nd and 101st Airborne Divisions were also dropped into the action on D-Day, but had been withdrawn earlier. The British 1st Airborne Division consisted of two parachute brigades (1 and 4) each of three battalions, an Airlanding Brigade, also of three battalions, and associated divisional support troops.

After the stagnant, static, set-piece trench warfare of the First World War, the Germans had introduced the concept of Blitzkrieg ('Lightning War') during the Second World War and established the Fallschirmjäger paratroopers as part of their arsenal to deliver it. General Kurt Student pioneered the use of German airborne forces in Norway and commanded them in France in 1940 and in the capture of Crete in 1941, the only completely successful strategic airborne operation of the war. Partly because of the high cost in casualties, the Germans mounted no further major airborne operations after Crete. However, their application was not lost on the British, particularly Prime Minister Winston Churchill, who recognised that a new type of war was being fought and ordered the creation of a new type of warrior to fight it. This included paratroopers, commandos, the Special Air Service (SAS) and Special Operations Executive (SOE), specialist combat units who were created, trained and deployed against the German Army. The paratroopers were not just infantry transported into battle by planes; they were specialist, elite soldiers, selected from the army and trained to operate behind enemy lines unsupported by heavy artillery and armour. They had to be tough, self-reliant and highly motivated and were tasked to carry out pivotal roles, vital to the success of the larger mission. Often spearheading crucial undertakings in advance of the main body, they were heavily relied upon to achieve their specific missions and most importantly could not be daunted if chaos reigned, as it inevitably would and most certainly did at Arnhem during Operation Market Garden.

Selected to deliver the 'Garden' part of the Operation was the Second British Army's XXX Corps (30 Corps) under Lieutenant General Brian Horrocks ('Jorrocks'), whose mother, Minna Moore, was the daughter of the Reverend J.C. Moore of Connor, County Antrim. XXX Corps was to move quickly up the 64-mile single-route axis over the airborne captured bridges to Arnhem to complete the surprise, shockingly spectacular bombshell of an operation. At its forefront was the Guards Armoured Division, commanded by Major General Allan Adair, with roughly 13,000 men and 200 tanks. Leading them, the first up the road, were the Irish Guards under the command of Lieutenant Colonel John Ormsby Evelyn 'Joe' Vandeleur.

Field Marshal Bernard Law Montgomery, the architect of Operation Market Garden, as well as Generals Horrocks and Adair and Lieutenant Colonel Vandeleur all had strong Irish connections, and there were many other such associations among the men of the US 82nd and 101st Airborne Divisions, both rank and file and in command positions. All those responsible, and those tasked to achieve individual objectives of Operation Market Garden, were substantially successful in their mission, but not enough to make the Operation the achievement it was hoped it would be. None more so than the men of the British 1st Airborne Division at Arnhem, and the whole would not prove to be greater than the sum of the successes of the plan's individual parts. For any of the many mentioned 'reasons' reached by historians, academics and commentators, Operation Market Garden failed to achieve its principal objective and many good men died. Mention Market Garden to the Dutch and they will tell you of 'the Battle of Arnhem and Oosterbeek'; the Germans will refer to it as 'The Cauldron'; whilst the Americans will respond with 'the Battle of Nijmegen'. Whatever it was called, the intent of the Operation was to finish the war in 1944, and had it succeeded it likely would have shortened the conflict.

To the British, Operation Market Garden had a deep, clear resonance of resolute resistance and resolve, an unswerving steadfastness and dogged determination displayed by the men of the British 1st Airborne Division at Arnhem. There they defended the north side of the Arnhem road bridge and the ever-shrinking perimeter in the western suburb of Oosterbeek. They confronted a German force far stronger than anticipated and bravely fought a highly-contested battle far fiercer and bitter than ever imagined. You cannot fight tanks and armoured vehicles with rifles and machine-guns, but for the most part they had to and did. By holding out with obstinate, unyielding, bloody-minded stubbornness, their wilful tenaciousness presented XXX Corps every opportunity to link up and consolidate the bridgehead, though 'time and space' abandoned them.

Among the British 1st Airborne Division at Arnhem were the Irish, well in excess of three hundred of them: the glider pilots and paratroopers; Pathfinders and Padres; in the glider-borne Airlanding (light) artillery, anti-tank and ambulances, reconnaissance and Royal Army Service Corps; also part of the signals and all other support elements of the Division. They were from a host of backgrounds, with a mix of experience and a range of ranks. Men from Northern Ireland and from the South, all members of an elite band of volunteer warriors distinguishable in the British Army by the coveted para wings, the airborne shoulder flash and the red (maroon) beret. However, the bond was not in the wearing of the insignia and the distinctive camouflage patterned smock, but what it signified; the camaraderie of being a soldier's soldier, of being among like-minded, highly committed, highly trained personnel with a carefully fostered fighting spirit and an acceptance of the highly dangerous role they were expected to perform.

1

MONTGOMERY'S AUDACIOUS PLAN

The rationale for the defeat of the full realisation of Operation Market Garden has been summed up, argued over and logically concluded by many historians as being for one, some, or all of the many following reasons: planning failures, ignored intelligence, the single axis, risk adversity, three airlifts, Panzer Divisions, bad weather, distant drop zones, no air support, for being overly optimistic, for meeting unexpected resistance, poor communications, the plans falling into enemy hands, bad luck and other 'cock ups'. There is some validity in each facet, more so perhaps in their combined collective causation, and yet despite these – ironically – the operation almost succeeded. British General Bernard Law Montgomery (Monty), the instigator of this imaginative, impressively simple and dramatically daring initiative, glossed over its defeat by saying it had been 'ninety percent successful', but Operation Market Garden undoubtedly failed to meet its end state; it didn't achieve its primary objective and was clearly not the success it was intended to be.

Many of the academic analyses, military after-action reviews and historians highlighting the misfortunes, mistakes, miscalculations and misconceptions of Operation Market Garden present us with a litany of oversights, omissions and outrageous planning decisions, yet at Eindhoven, Nijmegen and especially at Arnhem, the airborne soldiers and ground troops fought bravely, kept faith in themselves and performed proudly in adversity. To have baulked at the taking on of too much or to have been seen to prevaricate – despite one's individual innermost fears, doubts, anxieties and uncertainties in the atmosphere of optimism then prevalent – was simply not possible, as the currently assumed probability of being listened to was zero. Operation Market Garden was to be the knock-out blow on an enemy already 'staggering against the ropes', worn out, weak and demoralised, and if there was any element of chance involved then the disorganisation of the enemy demanded that risks be taken.

The prevailing circumstances made it possible, it was believed, to do just that – to end the war. However, opportunity is only as good as the use made of it, and when it is offered it needs to be taken before circumstances change. Hesitate and the opportunity is gone. That was how Field Marshal Montgomery, Commander of the British 21st Army Group (the land component commander for the invasion of North Western Europe), felt in early September 1944. 'Monty' was one of the best-known British Generals of the Second World War, distinctive in appearance and for his delivery of victory in North Africa over Rommel at the Battle of El Alamein (October–November 1942). From a family with deep roots in Moville, County Donegal, he was a professional and very serious-minded soldier who had seen service in the First World War, where he was decorated (DSO), shot and left for dead and returned determined that the army could do better, only to become posted to 'Rebel Cork' during the Irish War of Independence (1919–21).

As Brigade-Major 17th Infantry Brigade stationed in Victoria Barracks (now Collins Barracks), he considered its conduct worse than the Great War. A vicious, underground, counter-insurgency conflict of IRA ambush, Black and Tan reprisals and Auxiliary assassinations, he considered the execution of it 'lowered their standards of decency and chivalry' and was happy when the Truce came. At the outbreak of the Second World War, he commanded the 3rd Division in France in 1940 prior to the evacuation from Dunkirk (Operation Dynamo) of the last of the British Expeditionary Force (BEF) – over 225,000 men – brought back across the English Channel, the last to be successfully evacuated on 4 June 1940, leaving the Axis Powers to control the European continent and poised to invade England and Ireland. Major events since had propelled Monty to the fore in the war.

The momentum gained from D-Day had to be maintained after the hard fighting through the Normandy *bocage* countryside, a terrain of mixed woodland and pasture ideally suited to defence, and the dramatic collapse of German resistance. The Allied army advance on Paris and Brussels and the headlong retreat of the Germans convinced many that August 1944 was August 1918 all over again, the Allied offensive that ultimately led to the end of the First World War. Time, the dimension in which events continue or succeed one another, as well as being a measurement of moments passing in minutes and hours, is an element that military commanders need to be aware of, especially with consideration to its relationship with the space available, both that of the battlefield and areas of interest beyond it. Time and space are factors that commanders need to give careful thought towards in making a decision, and here in the prevailing circumstances along the Belgium–Netherlands border, the considerations of 'time and space' were best addressed by 'surprise and speed'. Monty felt airborne surprise in combination with the speed of XXX Corps were the key to success.

It was not, however, General Montgomery's decision to make, because on 1 September 1944 US General Dwight D. Eisenhower assumed direct command and operational control of all Allied ground forces in Europe. Montgomery was no longer the overall co-ordinator of the land battle, an appointment he had been granted by Eisenhower for the D-Day assault and the Battle of Normandy, thereafter. This, of course, placed American troops under Montgomery's command and back in the US public opinion turned against this, due to the already superior number of American troops in Europe and the ever-increasing US contribution of equipment and supplies to the Allied cause.

★★★

'Impracticable' had been Montgomery's immediate response when he first laid eyes on the proposed D-Day plan and he made essential revisions to it, including more troops and more space, as he rightly felt that the Allied assault needed to be strengthened and widened from three to five beaches and the inclusion of an additional air division. A successful invasion onto north western Europe was not the end state of Operation Overlord, but only the means by which it would begin. In light of his experiences in the stern school of active fighting, to achieve the wished-for outcome, the desired 'end state' is to be borne in mind from the very beginning; that it is a necessity to decide the development of the operation before ever initiating action, before troops ever cross the 'start line'. In other words, you must know strategically what you wish to achieve and how tactically it is to come about before you even begin the operation. It is essential to relate what is strategically desirable to what is tactically possible with the forces at your disposal.

With Hitler's 'Atlantic Wall' overcome in Normandy, the hard slog through the *bocage* countryside against fierce German resistance began. Montgomery's influence, direction and adherence to the plan was significant. His supervision and battle management, whereby the British and Canadian forces constantly engaged the German Army and drew in their reserves – more especially their tanks on the right flank of the Normandy Bridgehead – thus thinning, weakening and provoking gaps in the right flank, allowed the Americans to break-out. It had taken time but it had worked and the German collapse was staggering, and the Allied advance was swift.

The logistical pipeline is an operations lifeline. By late August, the Allied advance was in danger of overreaching what was physically possible to keep it supplied, particularly with ammunition and fuel. The advance was still being supplied from Normandy, but it had reached the limits of its exploitation and was having to slow down; in short, the lines of supply were overstretched. It had been Eisenhower's intention, insofar as he had a plan, to drive forward on a broad front, forcing the now unsettled Wehrmacht (German Army) to try to cope simultaneously with more than one threat. However, a lack of supplies meant that he was unable to exploit both US General Patton's advance in the south and Montgomery's in the north. Both had an intense dislike of each other and a long-standing rivalry existed between them – and each wanted to beat the other to Berlin.

Montgomery, now promoted by Churchill to Field Marshal, was highly conscious of time, and he knew that the momentum gained and maintained by the Allied advance would be lost because he believed Eisenhower would not concentrate his force, which could allow the Germans vital breathing space to reorganise; they were on the run and the pressure needed to be kept on them. Because Eisenhower had no plan, he devised one himself, a plan that would provide 'a really powerful and full-blooded thrust'. The stalling advance needed to be kept fluid but there was not enough fuel for both. Eisenhower could only support one – Montgomery or Patton – which was he to choose?

On 10 September 1944, Lieutenant Colonel 'Joe' Vandeleur was in command of the Irish Guards battle group consisting of the 2nd Battalion Irish Guards and 3rd Battalion Irish Guards. This group, with a Grenadier Guards group on its left, broke out of the Albert Canal bridgehead between Hechtel and Bourg-Leopold, directed on the Meuse–Escaut junction canal. Badly held up by the boggy and sandy terrain, late in the afternoon Lieutenant Colonel Vandeleur was forced to pass his group over the route taken by the Grenadiers, subsequently re-joining his own axis of advance. Once there he moved quickly and reached the neighbourhood of the canal at Overpelt, and moving westwards his force surprised the enemy holding the bridge at De Groote Barrier. With Infantry and sapper assistance he rushed across the bridge and under heavy covering fire from tanks he neutralised the German demolition charges on the bridge. Before the enemy even realised what was happening the Irish Guards armour streamed over the bridge, followed by more infantry.

> Lieutenant Colonel Vandeleur's drive and initiative in getting not only his tracked vehicles but also his infantry carrying lorries over appalling going and subsequently the speed of his advance when he at last reached a road, alone made the capture of the bridge possible. At

the bridge itself, his handling of infantry, tanks and sappers in intimate co-operation was a master example of how to force a crossing in the face of opposition. The feat was of quite outstanding influence in the course of future operations.

> *Citation for Distinguished Service Order (DSO) awarded*
> *on 1 March 1945 for action on 10 September 1944 to*
> *Lieutenant Colonel John Ormsby Evelyn Vandeleur.*

This action, the capture of what became known as 'Joe's Bridge', gave Field Marshal Montgomery his 'start line' for the beginning of the initially successful ground-based Allied assault: the push towards Arnhem named 'Garden', in conjunction with the airborne 'Market' campaign. Joe Vandeleur's great-great-grandfather, John Ormsby Vandeleur, was a British Army officer who fought in the French Revolutionary and Napoleonic wars. In 1808 he built Kilrush House on the 400-acre family demesne in Kilrush, County Clare, where the Vandeleur family had lived since the seventeenth century.

The concept of Montgomery's plan was to advance from Arnhem through the Ruhr to Berlin. Only to make that happen the Allies had first to get from Joe's Bridge outside Neerpelt, through Eindhoven and Nijmegen to Arnhem. This was the intent of Operation Market Garden, but the time and space available was very limited. The constraint on 'time' was twofold: could the Allies conduct a concentrated forward push into Holland with sufficient force before the Germans could reorganise themselves to put up any measure of meaningful defence; and if Operation Market Garden was implemented, could the effect of the surprise and speed of the attack sufficiently disorient the Germans for long enough before its effect wore off? The limitation regarding 'space' was also twofold: The principal restriction, of course, was space to manoeuvre, width-wise, left and right, from the single file one tank-breadth axis of advance over at least seven bridges; and then for the 64-mile distance to be completed within the time frame. The 'shock' of the airborne drops, and the 'awe' of XXX Corps' penetration behind enemy lines was the proposed answer.

The context of the preceding conditions and the current circumstances provided an optimistic frame of reference for the prevailing state of affairs. This tendency to take a more positive view of the situation arose from the collapse of German forces after the Allied break-out from Normandy and the relative effortlessness of their advance through northern France and Belgium to the Dutch border. The consequent sense of jubilation led to an almost delusionary and dangerous intoxication that the Germans had little left in terms of fight in them, and few resources to do so meaningfully. However, General Eisenhower had still to be convinced and time was passing. In addition, logistics were falling short. General Patton in the south was making demands and there remained no fundamental follow-up strategy or system laying out how the campaign was to be progressed after the break-out from Normandy. There needed to be an application of the fundamental principle of offence: the concentration of force onto one place at one time. Yet, instead of cohesion there was haphazardness and there was no single concerted effort. As a result, the focus was fragmented and the effort uncoordinated.

Eisenhower's headquarters at Granville on the west side of the Cherbourg Peninsula was perhaps suitable for him as Supreme Commander, but not so much for his position as land forces commander. Some 400 miles away and days out of touch with the land battle and his battle commanders, there were no telephone lines and not even a radio-telephone. Instructions, messages, directives and replies were delayed in being received and responded to, and it all prevented him from having his finger on the pulse of his armies and his ability to make quick decisions in rapidly-changing situations. All this 'looseness' in the posture of the Allied offensive was not conducive to timely and accurate estimates of the situation, much less quick decision making. None of it helped to eliminate the Allies having to face a long winter campaign.

Montgomery, conscious of the effect of five years of hostilities, much of it visited on a war-weary British population, had a greater sense of urgency to bring a swift end to the war. With this in mind he developed a plan codenamed Operation Comet. Although with the same strategic aims of the subsequent Operation Market Garden, Comet was a smaller scale operation in terms of troop deployment and would only be carried out by the British 1st Airborne Division and the Polish 1st Independent Parachute Brigade. However, several days of poor weather and concerns over increasing levels of German resistance persuaded Montgomery to postpone the operation, and finally to cancel it. Montgomery sought and received the opportunity of a meeting in Brussels with General Eisenhower on 10 September (1944). There he strongly put his case for an expanded version of Operation Comet, including the deployment of two US Airborne divisions. He laid out the concept of, for Montgomery, an uncharacteristically imaginative plan (normally he was known for favouring a methodical, almost punctilious, build-up of logistics and forces with very close attention to detail) and his reasons for it, stressing all the while that quick action was vital – every day the Allies continued in their current dispositions, they lost the 'go forward' initiative and gave the gift of time to the Germans. The freeing-up of the use of the port of Antwerp (the port itself was in Allied hands, the estuary in control of the Germans) would greatly alleviate the line of supply problems, so priority ought to be given to the northern front. He also presented General Eisenhower with information received from London the previous day concerning V-2 missile attacks on England; that these were being launched from sites in Holland, and he emphasised the importance of the early capture of the V-weapons launch sites in western Holland.

The optimum means to exploit the situation presented was one strategic bold, decisive blow, backed with adequate resources. This was far more favourable to a broad frontal advance, which without supporting supplies had to peter out at some stage, granting the Germans valuable time to reorganise their defence against the Allied advance. Montgomery's plan was to move forward on the northern flank and secure the Ruhr. In so doing there were major river obstacles – the Meuse, the Waal and the Neder Rijn (Lower Rhine) – and a number of man-made obstacles in the form of large canals. His plan was for the Allies to drive hard for the Rhine across all these obstacles and to seize a bridgehead beyond the Lower Rhine before the enemy could reorganise sufficiently to stop them. He wanted elements of the First Allied Airborne Corps allotted to him, placed under the command of the British Second Army Commander, another British general with Irish connections, General Sir Miles C. Dempsey.

The direction of the thrust would be towards Arnhem and the essential feature of the plan was the laying of a 'carpet' of airborne forces across the five major water obstacles which existed on the general axis of the main road through Eindhoven to Uden, Grave, Nijmegen and thence to Arnhem. General Horrocks' XXX Corps was to operate along the axis of the carpet then link up with the 1st British Airborne Division (part of the 1st Allied Airborne Army) in the Arnhem area and establish a bridgehead over the Neder Rijn north of the city. The Second Army was then to establish itself in the general area between Arnhem and the Zuiderzee, facing east, so as to be able to develop operations against the northern flank of the Ruhr. As XXX Corps moved northwards along the axis of advance, two other corps, VIII Corps under General Richard O'Connor on the east and XII Corps under General Neil Ritchie on the west, were to widen the axis of advance.

Eisenhower was thoughtful; he knew that the British manpower and economic situation was under severe strain and efforts to end the war in Europe before the end of 1944 were important both militarily and politically. However, he had 'politics' of his own to consider. Militarily, Patton on the southern front wanted to continue his advance into the German Saar area and he also had to bear in mind American public opinion. Still, the political situation favoured him being granted his lead, and 1944 was an election year in the US, so Eisenhower approved Montgomery's plan and allowed Operation Market Garden to enter the formal planning phase.

In September 1944, the Forward Edge of the Battle Area (FEBA) in north western Europe was the Belgian–Dutch border. Field Marshal Bernard Law Montgomery wanted it to be the Dutch–German border and he believed it strategically inadvisable to wait any longer. Hamstrung by an overextended supply line, the momentum of the Allied advance across north western

Europe was stalling and had to be curtailed. His worry was that if left too long this slowdown in the advance would allow the Germans time to regroup and reorganise a defence, and he wanted them kept off balance and 'on the run'. After a fiercely contested struggle through the *bocage* countryside of Normandy, the nature of their collapse had been staggering. It was such a dramatic disintegration that the mood among many on the Allied side was buoyant and upbeat. They were hopeful, indeed confident that an end to the war was likely before year's end.

Montgomery realised that this optimism had to be translated into a plan if the desired outcome was to be achieved. An opportunity now existed to deliver the 'knock out' blow, but the particular set of circumstances making this possible presently at hand would not remain in place for long; they had to act now. His concept of one concentrated, bold, penetrative and powerful push forward – a single knife-like drive into Arnhem towards Berlin – a concentration of strength with the essential elements of surprise and speed had been approved by the Allied Supreme Commander, General Eisenhower. The use of airborne troops dropped in a 'corridor' behind enemy lines combined with a simultaneous thrust northwards on the single axis of advance, linking up en route, was the straightforward scheme of manoeuvre, and being the biggest Allied operation since D-Day, it might just work.

'Plans are nothing but planning is everything' is a well-known military axiom. This generally accepted principle is a truism well digested among staff and field officers throughout the military for hundreds of years. The D-Day plan had been a masterpiece, involving much effort and difficulty; Operation Overlord was well considered and highly integrated, but it had taken months (some aspects of it even years). In contrast, the planning for Operation Market Garden would be barely seven days. In this sense, Market Garden was a gamble, not a risk. Military men take risks all the time, in conflict the exposure to harm, death and danger is intrinsic. Despite this, they are encouraged to be audacious, trained to be bold and even to aspire to be venturesome and daring; they never gamble. The difference is the judgement of being able to distinguish between the two: knowing when the degree of exposure to danger is being left to chance; deciding if the development of events without proper planning, or after well-considered alternative options, has been weighed against the likelihood of success and the optimum path chosen. To a military man the difference is obvious, the distinction immediately discernible.

This disparity had not gone unnoticed by many of the would-be participants of Operation Market Garden, but the prevailing mood of top-down optimism was such that it mitigated these concerns for the most part. The plan was seen for the opportunity it presented, and however scant the perceptions of poor planning were harboured individually, it sometimes represented the taking of the initiative. Its recognised value was of seizing the advantage inherent in the moment, and it was seen as the means of putting the Allies into a favourably positive position. Endorsed 'from the top', their task was to implement it and get on with the fighting. The entire concept was championed by those within the First Allied Airborne Army, whose greatest fear was not the opposition or the tight deadline, the monumental planning and preparation, the challenges presented by the mounting of the greatest paratrooper and glider-borne infantry operation ever conceived, but instead that it would be cancelled. Operation Market Garden was the biggest military gamble in history, driven by those responsible for its planning out of a primary priority that it would simply happen. On sixteen consecutive prior occasions, between June and September 1944, men of the First Allied Airborne Army had been 'stood to', in one case having actually emplaned, only to be subsequently 'stood down' because the speed of the on-ground infantry advance was such that it negated their planned deployment. Now, with the perceived end of the war supposedly close, there was an overwhelming ache to see action before it did end. These last-minute cancellations meant an ever-mounting frustration was palpable, and before this desperation dissolved into complete despondency, they wanted to put their boots on the ground and get into battle.

Only secondary and subordinate to this overriding worry were any concerns of evaluating the risks involved and their mitigation through proper planning. In Lieutenant General Hyde Brereton's (US Officer

Commanding First Allied Airborne Army) view, the issue as to whether it would be a day or night time drop was by far the most pressing issue, thereafter the prevention of the loss of aircraft was the next most troubling task. Not fully considered were the means essential to the preservation of two key elements crucial to the success of the plan: thunderclap surprise and facilitating the serious scope for speed. These and the road bridge at Arnhem were figuratively and literally lost sight of from an early stage. From south to north, firstly the 101st US Airborne would capture the bridges over the Wilhelmina and Willems canals at Son and Veghel in the vicinity north of Eindhoven. The US 82nd Airborne was responsible for the capture of the bridges over the Maas and Waal at Grave and Nijmegen. The capture of the last, and in many ways the most vital bridge, over the Neder Rijn at Arnhem was the responsibility of the British 1st Airborne with the Polish 1st Independent Parachute Brigade.

Immediately there was a difficulty: the achievement of complete and total surprise. The simultaneous dropping of three and a half airborne divisions to their respective designated drop and landing zones at the intended time on the same day was not possible because there were not enough aircraft available to make it happen. The planning was to go further astray due to RAF concerns over flak near Arnhem and Deelen airfield (ill-founded as it turned out), combined with concerns about the terrain near and to the south of the bridge, so drop zones no nearer than six to eight miles west of the bridge were selected. A self-inflicted loss of initiative from the get–go was apparent, and the advantage of surprise was severely compromised if not entirely lost at the operation's very beginning. The plan ceded to the shock value of catching the defence unaware; the gamble at Arnhem was becoming more apparent.

If there ever was a plan to ensure that a battle was over before it began and the battle lost before it could ever be won, surely it was at Arnhem. Only the men of the British 1st Airborne Division and the Polish 1st Independent Parachute Brigade did not know it yet. Aware of these and other difficulties, no efforts were made to invent, initiate or otherwise seek a fresh approach to forestall these problems. Lieutenant General Frederick Arthur Montague

'Boy' Browning, Deputy Commander First Allied Airborne Army was, before the war was over, all too keen to operationally command in battle the unit he had established. 'Three days of clear skies is all that was needed for Market Garden to be a success,' he stated to a briefing of his officers. In the event, the Allies were not even to get that.

2

BOUND FOR HOLLAND

The Holland-bound air armada was vast: British Horsa and Hamilcar gliders, together with US Waco gliders, named 'Hadrian' by the British, were towed by Albemarle, Halifax and Stirling 'tug' planes. Douglas C-47 Dakota transport aircraft full of paratroopers flew alongside, and the whole armada was protected by an escort of Lightning, Mosquito, Mustang, Spitfire, Tempest and Typhoon fighters. It inspired awe in all that were in it, saw it fly overhead or had to defend against it. The armada's military might was obvious and massive, its power potent and ferocious. It was sent to deliver specialist airborne soldiers to an unsuspecting German Army who were in for a shock, and a surprise.

The men on board the aircraft were committed to the mission. If any of them had or held any reservations about the plan they did not brood on them. From twenty-four airfields in England (eight British, sixteen American) they were launched skywards, the individual aircraft first forming into 'serials' and then into sky trains, in all massing into three immense columns above the English countryside. Two columns, the US 82nd Airborne and the 1st British Division, would take a northern route to Nijmegen and Arnhem, respectively. The US 101st Airborne took a southern route for Eindhoven. There was majesty in the armada's sheer overwhelming size, a resplendent gloriousness in its magnificence. A remarkable phenomenon to have seen, its thunderous roar could also be heard, 'as though an express train were passing overhead', according to Lieutenant General Horrocks as he waited with XXX Corps to advance.

By coincidence, 17 September 1944 was a Sunday and as the air armada headed towards the Netherlands special services were commemorating 'the valiant few' of the Battle of Britain, those RAF fighter pilots – no less than thirty-three Irish who died amongst them, the most famous being 'Paddy' Finucane from Dublin – who four years previously prevented the German Luftwaffe from gaining air superiority in advance of a potential German invasion of Britain (Unternehmen Seelöwe: Operation Sea Lion) and Ireland (Fall Grün: Case Green). Hitler then made the fatal mistake of turning east and invading Russia, opening up the Eastern Front. When the Allies subsequently opened up the Second Front into north western Europe on D–Day 6 June 1944, Germany – unable to sustain two campaigns – was in retreat on both. Now the ear-splitting tumult of the overhead aerial formations announced the Allied invasion of Holland.

The Allied 'Strategic Reserve', the newly-created entity that was the First Allied Airborne Army, was being put into the field and this new 'instrument of war' was being tested. It has been suggested since by some historians that deployment to assess its utility was the primary objective of Operation Market Garden, and that any success thereafter was secondary and a bonus. If it were, then it was also a means by which Field Marshal Montgomery thought he might regain control of Allied strategy (General Eisenhower having taken over as Allied Land Forces Commander on 1 September 1944). For General Dwight David 'Ike' Eisenhower, it was perhaps a way – if only for a while – to stop the bickering between his rival Generals seeking scarce resources. For General 'Boy' Browning, whose wife was the author Daphne du Maurier, it was a means to receive the much sought after (by him), role of finally commanding in battle a unit that he had helped to develop before the war ended, and the opportunity to do so ended with it.

With opportunity spoken of in terms of grasping the moment to maintain the forward momentum of the Allied advance, others perhaps saw within Operation Market Garden an opportunity of their own; a set of circumstances making it possible to do something favourable for themselves and reluctance to see the initiative framed in anything other than positive, even optimistic terms. There was nothing ambiguous in their ambition and their strong desire to achieve their own aims, hence there may have been a reason for so little regard paid towards the opposition. The German Army was painted as being under strength, worn out, without organisation and uncoordinated. It was described as badly rattled and incapable of mounting any meaningful massed defence, and for the most part consisted of old men and young boys with little equipment of note. However, what was known and what was said were different matters. Dutch underground resistance reports, air reconnaissance photographs and Ultra intercepts – the wartime signals intelligence obtained by breaking high-level encrypted enemy radio and teleprinter communications at Bletchley Park (the Allies had successfully broken the German secret 'unbreakable' Enigma code) – all pointed to the contrary, but this simply did not suit the narrative of the day and was not disseminated.

Military planning is based first and foremost on 'the threat' and the risks here were brushed over, whereas the norm is to consider the risks and if accepting them to make provision for them. Making no provision for the known risk made Operation Market Garden a gamble. Simply proposing the plan, getting it off the ground and executing it was considered enough, when really cognisance ought to have been given that in a fragile area, every action is a catalyst for another and the Germans were good soldiers. Hard fighting ahead ought to have been expected. As for the Allied soldiers en route, they were weighed down, tightly packed and for the most part relieved the Operation had not been cancelled.

Such an experience does not strike everyone the same way, however, and the exposure to potential imminent danger had different effects on personnel, both veterans and first-timers. Many were nauseous with airsickness, fear, or both. For some, this escalated into a deep dread and foreboding, an acute fear that left the sickening sensation of a lump of lead or a hollowness in the pit of their stomach, chronic dizziness in their head, and an inability to concentrate or hold any focused, coherent or rational thought for long in their minds. Overall, it presented a potential helplessness to react and overcome the challenge of their circumstances that threatened to overwhelm them to the point where they doubted themselves when their turn came to exit the aircraft. Losing their nerve, some American paratroopers pulled the ripcord of their reserve parachutes inside the plane to avoid jumping, hoping (or not) to later convince others that it was accidental and avoid a court martial charge of cowardice. Some veterans were were philosophical. Antony Beevor in *Arnhem, The Battle for the Bridges* (2018) relates that Staff Sergeant Russell O'Neal, a member of the US 82nd Airborne with three night combat jumps behind him, was inclined to believe that his 'Irish luck was about to run out'. When he received news that Operation Market Garden was a day drop he composed a letter to his mother that he subsequently did not send: 'You can hang a Gold Star in your window tonight mother. The Germans have a good chance to hit us before we even land.'

Then there were those who feared fear itself – the fear of feeling afraid is one of the biggest of all fears – and those who were worried about not measuring up to the demands of the circumstances. Stronger even than the fear of falling short of expectations was harbouring a strong sense of imminent death. There were those who held a presentiment that something was going to happen, a certainty of dying, while others reconciled to approaching death were fatalistic. That those with such premonitions contributed to their own self-fulfilling prophecy is unknown. Yet the vast majority sat there, waiting first for the red light to come on, then the green light, without overthinking the situation and waiting to see what the circumstance would bring when they literally hit the ground. Wedged in together and weighed down with equipment, they rationalised that the flight was only part of who they were and what they did, it was simply the means of getting themselves and their equipment to where they had to go, to do what they were trained for. On average, each man had to carry the equivalent of his own weight, so when the jump masters ordered the paratroopers to 'Stand up and hook up', even getting to their feet would not be easy. Each was weighed down by strapped-on equipment: their pack, bags, rations, grenades, first aid kits, water canteens and parachutes.

Ahead of them, Pathfinder paratroopers set off in twelve RAF Stirlings from RAF Fairford in Gloucestershire to act as navigators for the invading Allied troops. The 21st Independent Parachute Company, the elite of the elite, were heavily populated by the Irish: men like Privates James Fiely from Dublin and James Cameron from Carrickfergus, County Antrim, and Irish-born Lance Corporal Thomas Dunbar and Sergeant E.G.J. Cockings (both born in Ireland). Their task was to set Eureka homing beacons, coloured cloth strips and coloured smoke to mark the drop and landing zones for those about to arrive. For Operation Market Garden, they only had about twenty minutes to achieve their objective. The priority, of course, was to ensure the correct location was selected and, if necessary, fight off and defend against any enemy.

The orchestration of the air armada was carefully timed to coincide with earlier bombing raids of known German air defences. The route over Holland to Germany was well known to British and US bomber pilots, as it was the shortest route for Allied bombers heading to Germany. It was known by them as 'Flak Alley' because of the massive concentration of German anti-aircraft defences. Hence, the night before and in the early morning of 17 September 1944, 1,400 Allied bombers had taken off from British airfields and pummelled German airfields, anti-aircraft defence positions and barracks. Next, commencing at 0945 hours and lasting for over two hours, some 2,000 paratrooper transport planes, gliders and their 'tug' aircraft took to the skies and organised themselves into huge formations. The transports were joined by some 1,500 Allied fighters and fighter-bombers above, below and on their flanks, providing protection against enemy aircraft and supressing any anti-aircraft installations left undamaged by the earlier Allied bombing. In all, 4,900 aircraft were involved, the greatest number ever assembled on a single airborne mission. Between Bombing, Troop Transport, Protection and Resupply Taskings, it was undoubtedly an immense effort, a spectacular undertaking that could only be regarded with amazement.

Despite the prior bombing runs and a fighter escort, the pilots in the planes carrying or towing the thousands of Allied troops were still nervous as they flew over the North Sea. With the Dutch coastline in sight, it remained to be seen how effective the bombing of the German anti-aircraft batteries had been. As the gliders of the Airlanding Brigade crossed the Dutch coast in perfect formation, camouflage netting was pulled aside from hidden positions and the tops of dummy haystacks were removed to reveal concealed 88 mm guns and other anti-aircraft weaponry. Though most of the German flak batteries were subsequently destroyed by the RAF Hawker Typhoons escorting the gliders, the surviving guns managed to put up a barrage of what looked like black puffs of smoke. Only these flak shells contained shrapnel, which shredded the light fuselage of the gliders and accompanying transports, causing lethal injuries and wounding the helpless paratroopers and soldiers inside.

Lieutenant Colonel John Place from Foxrock, Dublin, Commanding Officer No. 2 Wing Glider Pilot Regiment, was the pilot of Horsa Glider 161. One piece of shrapnel from an exploding shell outside the cockpit window pierced the fuselage of the glider and fatally wounded co-pilot Ralph Alexander Maltby from Belfast, his body suddenly falling limp and lifeless. Lieutenant Colonel Place – who was map-reading at the time – took over piloting the glider and continued towards the Drop Zone, other members of the crew trying in vain to resuscitate Ralph Maltby. This, however, was not the end of their drama. As the glider neared its landing zone, machine-gun fire ripped through the plywood fuselage, smashing the knee of Private Hughes, a Bren Gunner of the Scout Section. Nevertheless, Lieutenant Colonel Place managed to bring the glider down in a safe and successful landing.

Antony Beevor in his 2018 book *Arnhem, The Battle for the Bridges* tells us that Lieutenant Colonel Patrick Cassidy, Battalion Commander of the US 1st Battalion 501st Airborne, sat opposite the Divisional Commander, Major General Maxwell Taylor, and was amazed at the latter's ability to sleep during the flight. He found it remarkable that the pilot managed to keep the plane on a level flight path, thereby allowing the paratroopers on board to jump, in the certain knowledge that every passing second further endangered himself and his crew. His attention focused on this drama, the illumination of the red, then green, lights in his own plane went unnoticed until he was alerted by the sharp tone of the now awake Divisional Commander: 'the green light is on!' He said, 'Yes sir!' and with his eyes still fixed on the nearby burning plane he jumped, followed by General Taylor.

North of them was Lieutenant General James 'Jumpin' Jim' Gavin, so named because he took part in the combat jumps with the paratroopers under his command. Of Irish parentage, 'Jumpin' Jim' Gavin was the youngest Major General, at thirty-seven, to command a Division. In all he was to complete four operational combat jumps during the Second World War and his orientation was strictly operational. Along with his personal sidearm he carried the infantryman's weapon, the M1 Garand rifle, not the M1 Carbine more usually carried by officers. He had also gained some prior notoriety because of his fight against segregation in the US Army. Sometimes called Slim Jim, he was commanding officer of the 82nd Airborne Division and for Operation Market Garden was responsible for the central sector in the vicinity of Nijmegen, and was charged with the seizure of the Maas and Waal crossings.

Born in Brooklyn, New York on 22 March 1907, details of his early years are unclear. His parents may have been Irish immigrants, Katherine Ryan and James Nally, but he was placed in an orphanage, the Convent of Mercy, when he was two years old. He was adopted by Martin and Mary Gavin in 1909 and from an early age was attracted to matters military and the commanding of troops in particular. Later, in Sicily, at Normandy (D-Day), in Arnhem and in the Ardennes (the Battle of the Bulge) he was certainly to do that – even fighting in the Korean War – and he earned a list of distinguished awards. Descending onto Dutch soil on this occasion, he hit the ground hard and fractured his spine, but Jumpin' Jim continued in his usual upright and forthrightly decisive manner.

For Private Patrick O'Hagan, also of the 82nd Airborne, the ill luck was reserved for his bazooka (a hand-held anti-tank weapon) team-mate.

Private First Class Belcher was among those convinced he was going to die, and he asked Private O'Hagan to make sure his girlfriend got his ring and Bible. True to his premonition, Pfc Belcher was shot in the air as he descended. Sergeant Charles Thomas Brackstone, twenty-three years old and from Dundonald, County Down, was co-pilot on-board Glider 319 of C Squadron, one of the larger British Hamilcar gliders. Having successfully landed their 8-tonne load (as opposed to the lighter, smaller 4-tonne load of the Horsa gliders) to Landing Zone S near Arnhem, he was killed by a burst of machine-gun fire while helping to unload his aircraft.

Given the size of the target and the number of flak positions to be flown over, despite the earlier bombing and the presence of the fighter escort and fighter-bombers, the casualties inflicted on the Allied air armada, the aircraft heading to Arnhem in particular, were slight. To have been one of them, or to have fallen victim to a crash landing on arrival, was all part of the cruel randomness of war. This arbitrary possibility and occasioning of ill luck had a finality to it and lives were lost. There were to be many more over the coming days.

3

THE OPERATION GETS UNDERWAY (17 SEPTEMBER 1944)

'Well, get a move on then.' The quietly-spoken words of command from Lieutenant Colonel 'Joe' Vandeleur, Irish Guards, to his lead tank commander, Lieutenant Keith Heathcote, to cross the 'start line' at Neerpelt and begin the advance of XXX Corps up the Eindhoven road set in motion the 'Garden' part of Operation Market Garden. The British XXX Corps needed to push through the German front line on the Belgian–Dutch border, and opposing them was 'Kampfgruppe (Battle Group) Walther'. With an approximate strength of 2,000 men, some sixteen anti-tank guns and heavy flak guns and howitzers, as well as a dozen or so Jagdpanzer IV tank destroyers (self-propelled anti-tank guns often mistaken for tanks), 'Walther' was an improvised battle group formed under Fallschirmjäger Colonel Erich Walther. The British XXX Corps commander, Lieutenant General Brian Horrocks, fully appreciated that firepower would be the decisive factor on the battlefield, and whoever brought it to bear most effectively usually won. Attack was all about firepower, momentum and timing; more precisely the accurate co-ordination of its moving parts at critical moments, and to inflict death, disorientation and disorganisation was the aim of artillery. Effectively executed, it is near to impossible to defend against, especially when there is enough of it, and the Allies had that.

This was an offensive manoeuvre without feint, deception or support; there was no pretence – it was simply to pulverise and penetrate. The plan was to pound and pummel the German line and create a hole in the line that the Allies could pour through toward their targets. There was no over-elaboration, the operation instead concentrating on a concerted artillery barrage and armour advance. A brutal bludgeoning, it was the application of direct offensive force to buckle and crumple the German line with the collective fire of 350–400 artillery pieces with a co-ordinated fire plan lasting thirty-five destructive minutes. It proved to have the desired effect, and the Allies succeeded in punching a hole in the German line and exploiting their forced entry with the Guards Armoured Division, the 'Micks' (Irish Guards) to the fore. This rapid deployment destroyed the German resistance, but characteristic of the Germans not without offering a fight. In all, their anti-tank fire knocked out nine British tanks.

The Allied artillery's rolling barrage from twenty regiments of medium and field artillery arched its fire onto a front 1,000 yards on either side of the Eindhoven road ahead of the Neerpelt 'start line'. The Germans referred to the (American manufactured) British Sherman tanks as 'Ronsons', because like the cigarette lighter of the same name they only had to strike them once and they lit up in flames, often resulting in the tank crews being burned alive inside. In typical British euphemistic understatement, the British themselves referred to it as being 'brewed up'. There is a savagery in war that is cruel, vicious and primitive, and the barbarity of the British artillery bombardment was no less brutal. The madness of it all, of course, was Hitler's refusal to accept the inevitable defeat facing him. His fanaticism was paid for with the lives of his soldiers, his people, and of course the lives of the Allied forces opposing him. With the sense that the war was all but won, with the Allies only waiting for it to be over, this understandably resulted in both a conscious and subconscious sensitivity (however sensible) to risk-adversity, an accusation sometimes made of the British by their American allies, and one instance whereby this might be considered was with the breakthrough achieved – time being of the essence – and the opportunity for speed accomplished, the British advance stopped seven miles up the Eindhoven road.

★★★

It was no surprise to the Germans that the Allies pursued a ground offensive into Holland; what did come as a shock was the deployment of the Allied Airborne Army Asset. The surprise the Allies had hoped to achieve was realised and the breakout through the thin crust of the German defence line on the Belgian–Dutch border was achieved; it now needed speed to capitalise on these successes, only the rate of acceleration of that time-sensitive advance was not apparent to all.

Kevin Myers in his Kinsale 2016 lecture on Irish participation in the British Army during World War Two noted that it is interesting to consider the thought-provoking aspects of the general picture of Irish involvement with the British during the war in relation to the numbers of Irish killed: over 170 Irishmen were killed with the Royal Armoured Corps, over 220 died with the Royal Engineers Corps and some 700 Irishmen died serving with the Royal Artillery. In fact, probably as many Irishmen died with 'the gunners' as with the so-called Irish regiments. For instance, even by the start of the war, under half of the Irish Guards were Irish and 30 per cent overall from the Republic. Over 800 Irish Guardsmen were killed, but only 250, a little over 30 per cent, were Irish, with just two-thirds from the Republic. So despite all the myths, the famous 'Micks' were largely British.

Other figures are equally surprising, if for different reasons. In almost all other British army categories, more men and women from the Republic than from the North were killed. Thus, eight southern Irish chaplains were killed compared to two Northerners. Fifty men from the south died in the Royal Army Medical Corps, compared to twenty-eight from the North. Of the thirty Irish nurses killed with the Queen Alexandra's Nursing Corps, twenty-three came from the South and it is worth bearing in mind that 16 per cent of all Queen Alexandra army nurses killed in the war were Irish. Fifty-three men from the South died in the Parachute Regiment, compared with thirty-five Northerners. Nearly 500 Irish-born British army officers were killed and over 70 per cent came from the South. Four Irish Brigadiers were killed, all from the South, and thirty-three Lieutenant Colonels were killed, of whom thirty were from the South. After 1940, all allegedly Irish regiments became predominantly British and simultaneously were opened up to more recruitment from the South of Ireland. By the end of the war, around 30 per cent of the dead of Northern Irish regiments were Irish with around 8 per cent from the South. Finally, just under 40 per cent of officers killed with Irish infantry battalions were in fact Irish, and 60 per cent of those Irish officers came from the South.

★★★

Only nineteen years old and already a Sergeant in the 3rd Parachute Battalion, Lawrence Lee from Castlebar, County Mayo, was preparing to jump on Arnhem as part of Operation Market Garden when he broke his foot playing soccer and was forced to stay behind. Staff Sergeant James Frederick 'Paddy' Boyd from Portstewart, County Derry, Squadron Quartermaster B Squadron, Glider Pilot Regiment was not selected to go on the Operation, but he was so keen to be involved that he stowed away on a glider, not wanting to miss out. Also not selected to go was 18-year-old Private Sam Kendrick from Bridgetown, County Wexford. A flamethrower operator in Assault Pioneer Platoon, 1st Parachute Battalion, he was initially considered too young to be sent on the operation but due to the absence without leave (AWOL) of the scheduled flamethrower operator he received approval to take the missing soldier's place only a few hours before lift-off.

On the same plane was Lance Corporal Mick Cox from Dublin, No. 1 Section 1st Airborne Provost Company (Military Police). A superstitious man, Mick was scheduled as number thirteen to jump and he was very unhappy about it, especially as no one would change with him. So instead he resorted to saying his prayers, over and over again, all the way to Holland. Private Norman Diffin, from County Armagh, of the 156 Parachute Battalion was badly wounded in another aircraft on its run in to the drop zone when flak (cannon shells) peppered the fuselage of the Dakota. The aircraft also crashed, and his combined injuries were so severe that he was medically repatriated with little delay.

Three sets of brothers from Ireland served and soldiered in Arnhem: From south of the border (County Dublin) were Private E.M. Conway,

Royal Army Medical Corps attached to 156 Parachute Battalion, and Lance Corporal J.J. (John Joseph) Conway, also 156 Parachute Battalion; and from Northern Ireland were Privates Francis and Thomas Dolaghan, in the 4 Parachute Brigade Headquarters, and Privates Robert 'Sandy' and Norman Dougan from Glenanne, County Armagh, both in R Company 1st Parachute Battalion.

It is instructive to follow what fate their individual involvements in Market Garden had ordained for them. First Sergeant Lawrence Lee's non-involvement due to a soccer injury saw him not fight at Arnhem with the 3rd Parachute Battalion, which as a unit was – amongst others – almost completely wiped out. He survived the war, went to live in Belfast and became a plant machinery driver. He married, had six children, and served in the Territorial Army Royal Engineers as a Company Sergeant Major for twenty-two years. The 'stowaway', Staff Sergeant 'Paddy' Boyd, was killed in action on the seventh day of Market Garden (23 September 1944) and is now buried in the Airborne Cemetery at Oosterbeek. Lance Corporal Mick Cox, 1st Airborne Provost Company, was captured and became a prisoner of war (POW). Private Norman Diffin, 156 Parachute Battalion, was severely wounded and medically repatriated to England. He recovered after a lengthy hospitalisation. Of the sets of brothers, the Conways from County Dublin were both captured and sent to the same POW camp, Stalag 11-B near Hammerstein; Francis Dolaghan, 4 Parachute Brigade Headquarters, was killed in action (KIA) on the second day (18 September) of Operation Market Garden and Thomas was captured and sent as a POW to Oflag XII-A, a German prisoner-of-war camp near Limburg an der Lahn. Of the County Armagh brothers, Robert 'Sandy' Dougan was one of the earliest casualties at Arnhem, killed on the first day (17 September) while Norman was one of the last to leave as he managed to evade capture and was to make it to freedom across the river Rhine in Operation Pegasus in November 1944. Returning to Glenanne after the war, he was unable to settle down and emigrated to Australia.

Fighting a losing battle for nine days, the experiences of these eleven soldiers were representative of what was tragically in store for the men of the British 1st Airborne Division at Arnhem. Many others would fight, kill and die; would wound and be wounded; and become casualties, prisoners of war or escapees across the River Rhine. Some would win awards for bravery, whilst others would see daring deeds go unrewarded. All would experience thirst, hunger and exhaustion in what would turn out to be a disastrous nine-day error-stricken engagement where 1,500 soldiers were killed in action, 6,500 became prisoners of war, and only 2,000 were able to return to the Allied lines – and then only just. And yet, because of the manner in which they fought, over 300 Irish amongst them, this military failure for the 'Arnhem men' became a source of pride to have been involved in and associated with. They substantially achieved their objective, held it for far longer than they ought, and gave the overall operation every chance of succeeding. These men played their part and did more than was asked of them in difficult, distressing and what became ultimately too dangerous a circumstance – humanly and militarily – to continue. They encountered far greater resistance than they were led to believe existed, and in the event this is how the first day of Operation Market Garden unfolded.

The planned suppression of the German defences by the British artillery Fire Plan having successfully taken effect, and with XXX Corps armour advancing up the Eindhoven road, the forward momentum for Lieutenant General Horrocks' breakthrough was being achieved. Encountering anti-tank ambushes as they moved forward, these were countered by the attention of Typhoon fighter-bombers of RAF 83 Group and 'Firefly' Sherman tanks with their 17-pound guns. Ahead of them, the Air Plan was in full swing and the airborne 'carpet' was being laid out: The gliders and paratroopers descending from the sky along the 64-mile 'corridor' to push open and keep open an axis of advance to Arnhem.

★★★

Upon landing, Lieutenant Colonel Patrick Cassidy became entangled in a barbed-wire fence, taking him some time and difficulty to free himself. The US 101st Airborne Division under General Maxwell Taylor reached most of its objectives by 1600 hours (4 pm), and the 101st Airborne secured bridge crossings at Heeswick, Veghel (501st Parachute Infantry Regiment) and Sint-Oedenrode (502nd Parachute Infantry Regiment), but the Germans blew up the bridge at Son over the Wilhelmina Canal as the 506th Parachute Infantry Regiment approached. An advance on an alternative bridge south of Best was blocked and Eindhoven itself not entered. Further north, the US 82nd Airborne Division under 'Jumpin' Jim' Gavin also had varied success. Grave Bridge was grabbed by the 504th Parachute Infantry Regiment while the Groesbeek Heights were seized by the 505th and 508th Parachute Infantry Regiments. Two of the three bridges over the Maas–Waal Canal were blown up by the Germans before the troops from the 504th and 505th arrived, and no move was made to seize the bridge at Nijmegen.

The fourth element of the Allied attack, the British First Airborne Division's simultaneous descent on Holland at Arnhem, the furthest Allied objective behind enemy lines, had begun in a promising fashion, likened for the most part more to an exercise than an operational drop. Overseen by the protective cover of members of the 21st Independent Parachute Company, they gathered themselves, shook out, formed up in platoon, company and Battalion RV and set about unloading their equipment. Their landing was a good one, it had been unopposed, the men were concentrated – not scattered and widely dispersed like the 6th Airborne Division at Normandy on D-Day – and there were very few casualties.

Inevitably there had been some injuries – and even fatalities – resulting from glider crashes or the noses of gliders getting stuck in ploughed fields on soft ground, the momentum of their landing tipping up the tail causing equipment and vehicles within to come loose and crush the pilot and/or co-pilot. There were accidental discharges from weapons – one Pathfinder paratrooper dropped his loaded Sten gun on landing and killed himself, and in two other cases rifles without the safety catches applied were being heaped onto trailers and went off, killing someone close by. There was even the unexplained occurrence of Private John Towhy from the South, found lying dead in the drop zone of No. 8 Section, 3 Platoon, R Company 2nd Parachute Battalion. Otherwise matters went smoothly, and after a while

– maybe slower than they should have – the Allied troops began to make their way towards Arnhem. Some eight miles away from the bridge, the British airborne troops approached in three columns along separate routes: Lion, Tiger and Leopard. Major Freddie Gough's Mobile Reconnaissance Squadron had gone on ahead, undertaking a dramatic 'dash for the bridge' in twenty-eight Jeeps with one Vickers machine-gun (K type) mounted on each Jeep.

Their arrival sparked delight amongst the Dutch population and there was an electric outburst of joy at what the occupied citizens believed was their liberation. However, if the local inhabitants' impromptu reaction had been to offer hugs, kisses, fruit and flowers, that of the genuinely surprised local German garrison – once they had gathered their wits – was resistance and an attempt to thwart the capture of what they quickly identified as the objective of the Allied Airborne attack: the bridge. This operation was best offered by blocking the British advance where it was most advantageous, and a rapid series of defence lines were organised on the routes leading in from the west of the city where the drop zones were located. The scene was set for the initial skirmishes, which would quickly develop into shoot-outs and, from the German perspective, the hopeful slaughter of the foreign Allied Fallschirmjägers (paratroopers). They were well equipped and German resistance was to come as an unwelcome surprise to the men of the British 1st Airborne Division.

These Kampfgruppe (battle group) formations of varying sizes of manpower and machinery (armour and artillery) were created out of necessity as a means to offer an improvised defence. Two weeks earlier, arriving in northern Belgium and disregarding orders to move his troops to the Rhineland to rest and reorganise, Generalleutnant Kurt Chill instead deployed them along the north bank of the Albert Canal. Here he established checkpoints, halted and gathered together all German personnel and organised them into units. Two days later (7 September) Chill was allocated reinforcements by Generalleutnant Hans Reinhard. Hitler, reacting sternly to the capture of Antwerp on 4 September, appointed Generalfeldmarschall Walter Model as Commander of Group B to defend

Holland and northwest Germany. Known as 'the Führer's fireman' he had earned his reputation on the Eastern Front, displaying an ability to turn around Russian routes into viable German counter attacks, and this ability was clearly needed in Holland. Generalfeldmarschall Gerd von Rundstedt was appointed Oberbefehlshaber West or OB West (Commander in Chief West), and looking for somewhere safe, quiet and out of the way had selected at random Arnhem for the withdrawal of SS-Obergruppenführer Wilhelm Bittrich's Panzer Group. Model himself set up his headquarters in the Hartenstein Hotel in Oosterbeek, a western suburb of Arnhem.

The new dispositions, increased troop numbers, armament, equipment and command structure was highly fortuitous for the Germans and entirely regrettable for the Allies. For the Allied planners of Operation Market Garden, the enemy situation of their considerations had changed quite dramatically, but their plan had not changed one iota … and into this battle space, in the biggest operation since D–Day, dropped the British 1st Airborne Division. When attending the briefing given by British Lieutenant General 'Boy' Browning on 10 September – when Browning unveiled the plan's concept – Major General Stanisław Sosabowski, Officer Commanding 1st Polish Parachute Brigade attached to the British 1st Airborne Division, had asked: 'The Germans … what about the Germans?' Little mention was made of the potential opposition the Allies were likely to encounter, but they would have done well to have paid heed to Major General Sosabowski, as there is nothing more vulnerable or vicious than an army in retreat.

★★★

Strength, surprise, speed and support – key elements for the airborne plan's success – had all been severely hampered by a lack of detailed planning and the time given to consider such important matters. In addition, the priority given to the Air Plan against the overall purpose of the mission was confused, and the strength of the British Airborne Division fragmented by an insistence they be inserted over three days. The option to undertake a two-lift one-day turnaround on the first day was dismissed too easily, when its feasibility was not as unworkable as was suggested. The requirement to provide security for the landing and drop zones further diminished the strength of the initial day's attack. Finally, the allocation of thirty-five gliders to General Browning's HQ could have been more pragmatically utilised to bring in more troops, ammunition and armaments. The element of surprise was also severely diluted by choosing landing and drop zones too far from their objectives. The Allies were only going to get one chance to benefit from a surprise assault and this was lost all too easily, for little gain. Speed was compromised by wasted time in forming up; the vehicles landed by glider while the Reconnaissance Squadron personnel were parachuted in and it took two and a half hours for the supposed 'dash to the bridge' to get underway from the drop zone. Finally, a directive not to allow close air support by Allied fighter and fighter-bomber aircraft into the same airspace as used for the Allied air drop and resupply denied the lightly armed paratroopers vital firepower support.

Lost also, as it happened, were radio communications, the Divisional Commander from his headquarters, a set of the Operation's plans which fell into German hands, the Allied use of the resupply zone, and the weather window – delaying troop drops on the second and third days. Poor planning, poor weather and poor luck meant matters did not go favourably when the British Airborne Division most needed them. Of all operations, it was important that the Allies 'take their chances early', because the odds were diminishing with every hour that passed without gains being made. The use of a lightly-armed paratrooper force for rapid deployment is attractive, but if they are unsupported their ever-diminishing resources leave them vulnerable, especially in relation to a defender's ability to receive increasing numbers of reinforcements, In a short time, the resources ratio can quickly favour the defenders – paratroopers on their own cannot fight for long and if isolated they are lost. One amongst the German generals present, General Kurt Student, the pioneer of the use of airborne forces who had commanded them in France and in the capture of Crete, knew this well.

The die was cast; the Germans had the strength, armament, and experienced commanders. If they could get their forces in and around the

Arnhem area physically positioned between the bridge and the approaching British Airborne with some degree of cohesion they could significantly hamper the attack. These were tense times. For the British Airborne, if the battle was to be won the last chance of success was contingent on the surprise achieved here and now, on Day One, when the German Army's confusion, disorganisation, and demoralisation was at its highest and the initiative was still with the attacker. The outcome of the battle would hinge on the early actions and reactions of attackers and defenders respectively, and whosoever could wrestle the initiative from the other and gain the position to forestall the other's intentions would likely win. They just needed to execute the Plan accordingly and early and they would become a real and deadly thorn in the side of their opposition. Moving into action, the 1 Parachute Brigade of the British 1st Airborne Division proceeded to Arnhem via three routes: Lieutenant Colonel David Dobie's 1st Battalion along the north, Leopard route; on Amsterdamseweg, Lieutenant Colonel John Dutton 'Johnny' Frost's 2nd Battalion along the south, Tiger route; and Lieutenant Colonel John Fitch's 3rd Battalion down the main Utrechtseweg road, on the Lion route. Accompanying them were the 1st Airborne Brigade HQ and out in front Major Gough's 1st Airborne Reconnaissance Squadron.

The 'patient determination to kill' is the military definition of an ambush, and Major Freddie Gough's 1st Airborne Reconnaissance Squadron drove straight into just such a circumstance. A well laid out and properly set Germans ambush, concealed and armed with mortars and machine-guns, fired upon Major Gough's jeeps soon after they crossed the railway line in Wolfheze. The dash was halted, and whoever was going to reach the bridge first would have to do so on foot. Meanwhile, the three battalions each proceeded to probe a passage through the outskirts of the city's suburbs, meeting resistance whichever way they went. No. 9 Platoon of C Company, 2nd Parachute Battalion under Lieutenant Peter Barry, closely followed by No. 8 Platoon, managed to successfully close in on the railway bridge, and its capture by them was looking decidedly possible only for it to be blown up with some of his men on it. Lieutenant Barry was badly wounded and carried to safety by his platoon sergeant. He was convinced that had they been landed on the fields between the railway bridge and Oosterbeek, never mind about the flak, it would have been there for the taking. It was a bridge that an army could have got tanks and everything else across, but they had landed in the wrong place and the Germans had three hours warning.

The forewarning of the Allied Airborne attack on the bridge was to see the Germans use to very good effect their six-barrelled rocket launchers, nicknamed 'Moaning Minnies' for the distinctive sound they made. Not only did these rockets wreak havoc when they landed, but their fearful noise had a debilitating effect also. Cork-born Major Mervyn Dennison, Commander of A Company, 3rd Parachute Battalion, and his men bore the full brunt of their force as the Moaning Minnies filled the air with their frightful banshee-like screaming, shrieking and screeching. Dispersal of his troops was the answer, and the successful 'putting in' of platoons to attack the nearby water tower being used as an observation post (OP) by the Germans. Full-blown firefights broke out all along the Airborne's forward advance, the soldiers on both sides becoming engaged as the British found their way blocked and their advance halted. Attempts to outflank the Germans were to no avail, and having entered into contact with the enemy it was important to win the firefight to force the assault, be it in front or from the flanks, but the Airborne's weight of numbers and of fire was simply insufficient. Nor were the numbers of attackers to defenders, in terms of their attempts to break through to the bridge, going to get any more favourable.

Lieutenant Colonel Frost's 2nd Parachute Battalion, advancing along the River road, was progressing successfully but not entirely without incident, either. The troops came under fire from a concealed German machine-gun position and a number of their mortar platoon were wounded. Lieutenant Reginald Bryan 'Danny Boy' Woods, from Malahide, County Dublin, Platoon Commander Mortar Platoon, gave covering fire from the centre of the road with his pistol while the remainder of the platoon, heavily laden with ammunition boxes, mortar barrels and base plates, scrambled into cover. They moved through the suburbs and into the town, and as dusk approached a blast of machine-gun fire with tracer suddenly burst across their front. Lieutenant 'Danny Boy' Woods ordered up the platoon's Bren gun carrier, and together with his driver made a headlong drive straight into the gunfire, his machine-gun blazing. A 'no holds barred' duel erupted between the two sides until one was silenced. The German machine gunners were killed and his platoon was safe again.

As the 2nd Parachute Battalion made for the Arnhem road bridge, the main German blocking line was thrown across the British axis of advance just after A Company had made its way to the bridge. Meanwhile, with the railway bridge blown C Company under Major Dover made for their secondary objective, the German headquarters in Nieuwe Plein. Already, German resistance was increasing both in numbers of men and the addition of self-propelled assault guns and armoured cars. One such vehicle, an armoured half-track with a 75 mm gun, drew close to C Company's position and its shelling was causing casualties. The lead platoon commander, Lieutenant I.A. Russell, called forward Private William (Billy) Saunders, from Belfast, and ordered him to bring his mortar into play against the vehicle. The range was too short for a mortar's indirect fire, but Private Saunders had an unconventional solution. Placing extra shell dressings as padding on his right shoulder as a cushion to offset the recoil of the mortar, he lay against the side of a ditch and aimed the mortar tube towards the half-track as a makeshift anti-tank weapon. It took two rounds, the first went high but the second hit the armoured cab of the half-track. The crew surrendered, but no further movement was possible for C Company, 2nd Parachute Battalion that night.

Also contained in their advance were the 1st and 3rd Parachute Battalions. Only the 2nd Parachute Battalion (minus C Company) arrived to the bridge, amongst them Father Bernard Egan, the Battalion Padre, Lance Corporal Daniel Neville, from Listowel, County Kerry, a member of the 1st Parachute Squadron Royal Engineers, Private Cecil Newell from County Down, and the red-haired, Irish-born Sergeant Mulhall. The Battalion proceeded to occupy buildings around the north end of the bridge, and all told it was a contingent of a 'battalion plus' strength that held their objective. C Company of the 3rd Parachute Battalion managed to get through, as did Major Freddie Gough with three jeeps from Reconnaissance Squadron and 1st Airborne Division Headquarters (minus the Division Commander, but importantly with radios). Two unsuccessful attempts were made during the night to secure the southern end of the bridge, after which the 2nd Parachute Battalion settled down for an uneasy night.

Speed: the rate at which the 1 Parachute Brigade moved; distance: the space between the landing zones and the bridge; opposition: the level of resistance offered by the Germans. These were the variables at play at Arnhem on the first day of Operation Market Garden. As if to emphasise that it was important to make the most of the opportunity that their surprise arrival offered, Lance Corporal Mick Cox and the eleven men of No. 1 Section 1st Airborne Provost Company marched unopposed into Arnhem, moving directly and at speed to their objective, the Police headquarters, and achieved their task. His host of 'Hail Mary's' whilst seated at position number thirteen on the Dakota was seemingly answered.

4

TRAPPED IN ARNHEM
(18 SEPTEMBER 1944)

Major Mervyn Dennison commanded A Company of the 3rd Parachute Battalion which had been dropped west of Arnhem on 17 September 1944. During the advance on the town on the evening of 17 September the Battalion was held up, and shortly afterwards Major Dennison's Company in the rear came under small arms and heavy mortar fire from the flank. Major Dennison led two platoons of his Company and overran three enemy machine-gun posts which formed the nucleus of the opposition on the flank. On the following morning Major Dennison's Company acted as a rear-guard to the Battalion advance on Arnhem, but was cut off from the remainder of the Battalion by strong enemy forces. Later the Battalion got into serious difficulties and Major Dennison, with reserve ammunition, was ordered to fight his way through at all costs. This he did successfully against very strong opposition. Throughout both these actions Major Dennison showed a high standard of personal courage, leadership and determination. Even when severely wounded in both arms, he continued to encourage and inspire his men.

Citation for Award of the Military Cross.

The reality of the situation on the ground at Arnhem was somewhat different to the expectations of the British Airborne Division. They found their way to the bridge blocked and their efforts to move the point of attack left them in 'contact' situations where the fire fights were unequal. Progress was paralysed, they could not find a way past, through or around the German blocking lines. The element of surprise was now lost, and lacking in strength the operation was beginning to misfire. Although diminished since Normandy, the fighting capacity of the two Waffen-SS Panzer Divisions present in Arnhem required something extra from the lightly-armed British troops that was difficult to find – the dominant strength and control of the German armour proving impossible to counter.

In a straight shoot-out situation, which the confrontation in Arnhem was rapidly becoming, the Allies were simply outgunned. Disorientated and disquieted by a German defence that was not supposed to exist in anything like the extent that it did, the British were increasingly frustrated, tired and not a little fearful at where they found themselves. Communications were malfunctioning, command and control was proving difficult, and cohesion was threatening to fragment. Co-ordination of the efforts of the individual parachute battalions in any linked-up concentration of force was eluding them. However, the Airborne Division were not regarded as the elite for nothing and a reinvigoration of their positive psyche was an essential part of their superiority – that and courage and a direct approach.

At dawn on the second day the British applied pressure to the German blocking lines. Meanwhile, the Germans applied force of their own and made a move against the landing zones west of Arnhem, both by air and ground attack. Lieutenant Colonel Frost's 2nd Parachute Battalion 'stood-to' at the bridge, waiting for the inevitable German counter attack. The Battalion had successfully reached the northern end of the bridge, the Germans arriving in their wake having only assembled their blocking line following the Battalion's infiltration, but the southern end of the bridge was still held by the enemy. This meant that with Germans both ahead and behind them the Battalion was surrounded and cut off from the rest of the 1st Airborne Division. Lieutenant Colonel Dobie's 1st and Fitch's 3rd Parachute Battalions had been halted and pinned down by enemy blocking lines formed of a mix of hastily cobbled together *ad hoc* combinations, which varied between non-infantry Luftwaffe airmen and crack SS Panzergrenadiers. Anyone and everyone had been hurriedly scrambled and rushed into the blocking lines.

Major General Robert Elliot Urquhart, British 1st Airborne Divisional Commander, had gone forward to get a front-line view of what was happening and had eventually met up with Brigadier General Gerald Lathbury, British 1st Airborne Brigade Commander, and they had attached themselves to the advance of Fitch's 3rd Parachute Battalion. Major General Urquhart may have felt otherwise, but he was not where his duty (or the situation) required him to be: his Divisional Headquarters. The Battalion first encountered isolated harassing sniper fire, followed by machine-gun blasts, then mortars and finally shell fire from armoured cars and self-propelled anti-tank guns. Surviving 20 mm anti-aircraft guns were also deployed, and were used horizontally in a ground fire role against the advancing British troops.

Back at the landing zones, the British glider-borne Airlanding Brigade under Brigadier Philip 'Pip' Hicks, consisting of 1st Battalion Border Regiment, 2nd Battalion South Staffordshire and 7th Battalion King's Own Scottish Borders (KOSBs) along with the 21st Independent Parachute Company, were securing the landing and drop zones for the Second Lift (composed mostly of the 4 Parachute Brigade, expected during the morning of Day Two). Meanwhile, the 1st Airlanding Light Regiment, Royal Artillery, were setting up their 75 mm Howitzers close to Old Church at Oosterbeek. Among them were Gunner Joseph Doran from County Donegal, Sergeant John Joseph Daly from County Waterford, Gunner M. Cooney from Dublin, Lieutenant Donald Siggins from Portrush, County Antrim, and Gunners Thomas Hamilton from Dollingstown, County Antrim, E. Williams from Omagh, County Tyrone, and F.W. Vint, who received a mention in dispatches.

Trapped in Arnhem (18 September 1944)

The men of the British Glider Pilot Regiment, the pilots and co-pilots, were trained to fight alongside the British Airborne Units once they had landed their gliders (not so in the US Airborne) and at Arnhem they formed two 'wings', each the equivalent of a battalion, and contributed hugely in the fighting. In all, there were 1,200 men of all ranks such as Staff Sergeant Brian Patrick Sheridan Feehily, Sergeants J.A.B. Wetheral from Blackrock, Dublin, Thomas John Duncan Simpson from Belfast, Eric George Wolf Masterson from Bandon, County Cork, and D.S. Parker from County Cavan. Irish officers included Lieutenants G.R. 'Dusty' Millar from County Cork and Ralph Maltby from Belfast (killed by shrapnel at the controls of Glider 161), Lieutenant Colonel J.W. Place from Foxrock, Dublin, and Regimental Sergeant Major Michael Briody from County Kilkenny, amongst others.

Meanwhile, back in England matters were not going to plan either. Fog delayed the deployment of the Second Lift by some four hours. This consisted mainly of the 4 Parachute Brigade under Brigadier General John 'Shan' Hackett, with the 10th, 11th and 156 Parachute Battalions. Further bad weather en route deterred a sizeable portion of the Second Lift from proceeding, and those who did persist received a far more hostile reception from the Germans on arrival than expected. Thanks to the capture of a set of Operation Market Garden plans, the Germans were now aware of the location of the landing zones and this allowed them to better site their anti-aircraft weapons. Nonetheless, British reinforcements were successfully landed. In far greater numbers, German reinforcements began to arrive to the battle space, crucially including tanks amongst its arsenal. The stipulation by Major General Paul L. Williams, USAAF IX Troop Carrier Command, one of the Air Elements of the First Allied Airborne Army (the other two being RAF 38 Group and RAF 46 Group) that Allied fighter and fighter-bomber support aircraft in Belgium remain grounded while his own were flying meant a loss of Allied air superiority. Instead of the British 1st Airborne Division being able to avail themselves of an important asset of air firepower to help break deadlock situations, protect troops and press home their advantage, the Allies were left unprotected and prone to attack by an increasingly powerful German Army. Never expecting to hold all the aces, on-ground commanders do the best with the situations that arise, but so many of the disadvantages they had to cope with were unnecessarily self-inflicted by prescriptive, precipitous and ultimately poor planning.

As the skirmishes of the first day drew to a close, Day Two saw far more serious exchanges erupt simultaneously on the western landing zones, in the town's suburbs and on the road bridge. Not only were the actions concurrent and concentrated, the fighting involved had a characteristic all of its own, for which airborne troops were untrained. This was urban territory, street warfare and fighting in built up areas – a different type of hostility to green-field, conventional combat which requires different skills, training and techniques. Urban combat is three dimensional, it can take place at ground level, above ground in buildings and even below ground at basement, even sewer level. It is heavier in casualties and much more demanding of ammunition. It literally goes from street to street, house to house, floor to floor, room to room, man to man in hand-to-hand fighting. When negotiating a built-up area on the advance, a commander's first and instinctive choice is to bypass and isolate, secondly to stand off and bombard, and only finally – if there is no other alternative – go in and fight. Apart from a question of tactics, it is expensive not only in manpower and ammunition, but time and logistics too.

The circumstance in which the British Airborne Division now found themselves, instead of a supposed clean sweep to victory and quick possession of the river crossing, was to grind out any gains the hard way, one street at a time. It was a much tougher challenge, and a failure to generate the forward momentum expected had placed them on the back foot. But could they still come out on top? One thing for sure was that the Germans were not going to hand the Airborne Division victory on a plate; they would have to take it themselves. So it was 'get up and go' time and both the 1st and 3rd Parachute Battalions did just that.

When fighting in built-up areas, the 'front line' becomes confused and can overlap and intermingle on and along parallel streets; gains may be made on one street while the enemy advances on another. Counter attacks can occur and the situation can easily become mixed up, messy and complicated. Typically involved in attempting to gain forward movement was Cork-born Major Mervyn Dennison's A Company, 3rd Parachute Battalion. As the Battalion was engaged in its attempted advance, A Company became detached and separated. Both A Company and the Battalion itself became ceaselessly machine-gunned and mortared. The noise was both debilitating and deafening: the rattle of machine-guns, the impact of mortars, and the reverberation of shell blasts from armoured cars and self-propelled Sturmgeschütz assault guns (Stugs) as they ripped through trees and walls, causing explosions and fireballs.

'Crump, crump, crump,' the incoming mortar rounds slammed into the streets, and it took only a short time for their fire to smash into A Company's position. The ground shook with each blast, walls were fragmented, bricks shattered, and hot molten shrapnel indiscriminately spread in search of victims. Major Dennison was caught on the wrong side of one such mortar barrage and knocked unconscious. As he came too he witnessed small-arms confrontations between rival groups of British and German troop sections, moving forward and back, taking cover and re-emerging, taking firing positions. The opposing forces were playing a deadly game of 'cat and mouse', firing at each other, taking cover and then chasing one other.

Before he knew it, and only barely awake, Major Dennison was confronted by a bayonet-wielding German rifleman and engaged in close combat with him, receiving bayonet wounds to both hands. The assailant was quickly killed by another member of the Company coming to Major Dennison's defence. It was all very ugly, raw and horribly violent; a response to brutal force with close-quarter savagery. Tasked to get much-needed ammunition forward with other supplies to the Battalion's troops fighting in the vicinity of the St Elisabeth Hospital, Major Dennison loaded the remaining Company Bren gun carrier under the supervision of a 'stray', Lieutenant Burwash of B Company, and on its arrival was welcomed by the remnants of 3rd Parachute. The ammunition and supplies were immediately distributed and utilised by the Battalion whilst under constant attack, enabling them to hold their ground – just. Major Mervyn Dennison was to receive the Military Cross (MC) for his actions at Arnhem.

Also under mortar bombardment was the Jeep of Major General Robert Urquhart, Commander 1st British Airborne Division. He and Brigadier General Lathbury, 1 Parachute Brigade, were to find they had become separated in the middle of the melee and the disorder, and were now themselves cut off and surrounded by Germans. Lathbury was wounded and left in the care of sympathetic locals in a nearby house while Urquhart took shelter, hiding in the attic of another helpful local, and was both out of touch with the battle and out of reach of Divisional Headquarters. Brigadier General Philip 'Pip' Hicks, Officer Commanding Airlanding Brigade, had now to take over temporary command of the Division and attempt to co-ordinate the management of some form of shape onto a quickly deteriorating, changing and problematic situation. With the mid-afternoon arrival of the Second Lift, he had at least the infusion of Brigadier Hackett's 4 Parachute Brigade, some 2,000-plus troops, to add to the 5,000 already arrived and deployed the previous day. The 11th Parachute Battalion and South Staffordshire Regiment were immediately sent to reinforce the 1 Parachute Brigade's attack, hoping to influence the battle and prevent matters from falling into total disarray.

Relatively speaking, Lieutenant Colonel 'Johnny' Frost's 2nd Parachute Battalion was in a reasonably strong position to hold as they were, for a while anyway. They had occupied a perimeter of some twenty buildings at the northern end of the road bridge and now found themselves holding out against multiple German assaults, both from the southern end of the bridge and encroaching around the periphery of their position. In a somewhat bizarre early-morning assault, a rag-tag convoy of twenty-two armoured cars, open half-trucks and trucks protected only with sandbags of the 9th SS-Aufklärung-Abteilung (reconnaissance battalion) attempted a reckless full speed charge across the bridge, with fatal results. The debris of the bullet-riddled, burned-out vehicles ended up littering the bridge's roadway at the northern end. The commander of the ill-fated attack, SS-Hauptsturmführer Viktor Gräbner, who had received the Knight's Cross the previous day for his actions in Normandy, was killed in the attack. Next, the buildings on the battalion's perimeter became contested for and the fighting was close-up to the point where the soldiers in a school building occupied by a detachment of Royal Engineers (the sappers) under Captain Eric Mackay, with Lance Corporal Daniel Neville from Listowel, County Kerry, among them, dropped grenades out of the window to fend off German attackers only metres away.

Realising the British paratroopers were a determined force, the Germans opted for a more methodical approach: to stand off and blast their way in, systematically destroying each of the British-occupied buildings from the top down with artillery and armour fire. With the fighting inevitably came casualties, and the attrition rate and wearing away of British numbers gradually diminished their fighting capacity. Arriving into 'the Cauldron' came Hackett's Brigade, more Irish amongst them, but in far superior numbers German reinforcements arrived too. German tanks, including Tigers from the Knast Kampfgruppe, arrived by train on the Blitztransport, special train services for the movement of personnel and equipment directly to their destinations from all across Germany.

In contrast, the progress of XXX Corps up the Eindhoven road was pedestrian by comparison. Now clear of German troops, the armoured column reached the destroyed bridge at Son without incident, and further progress was now dependent on the speed of XXX Corps bridge builders. In the event it was to take ten hours, meaning that as the armoured column was crossing the following morning, they were already a day and a half behind schedule. Ahead of them, the US 82nd Airborne was attacked on the Groesbeek Heights but held their position. The Germans were also holding the bridge at Nijmegen, despite three attempts to take it from them, as they had identified that river crossing as key to the overall battle: deny the Nijmegen bridge to the Allies, halt the advance of the British XXX Corps and whatever happened at Arnhem was academic. The Germans were also organising to launch assaults against the corridor and cut the route at Veghel, as it was favoured by them as being a vulnerable point because the corridor there was narrow and so a choke point.

By the end of the second day, it was clear that the German opposition at Arnhem had been underestimated, the British were untrained for street fighting, and the speed at which the Germans could bring in reinforcements had been unimagined. The signs were ominous for the British, but they only had to hold until XXX Corps arrived and with no communications to the contrary (they had no communications at all) they were blissfully unaware of the delays and difficulties XXX Corps was facing. Equally uninformed of the Allied predicament at Arnhem were XXX Corps and General 'Boy' Browning's headquarters. In the absence of any other information, each assumed all was going to plan. Meanwhile, it was obvious to Lance Corporal Mick Cox and his cadre of Military Police at Arnhem Police Station that despite being in the midst of the mayhem the Germans were unaware they were there. That the Germans remained uninformed was too much to hope for, or was it?

5

THE ENEMY REGROUPS (19 SEPTEMBER 1944)

Moving at pace, the speed of the small convoy through the Dutch countryside conveyed the urgency of their task. The British supply drops were going astray and the sustainability of the Operation was beginning to be put in jeopardy. Travelling at speed, the cavalcade of four jeeps complete with trailers was manned by over twenty men commanded by Irishman Captain Desmond Kavanagh from 2 Parachute Jeep Section, 2 Parachute Platoon of the 250 (Airborne) Light Composite Company Royal Army Service Corps. They had left the British Airborne Landing Positions west of Arnhem and were heading towards a pre-designated Supply Dropping Zone approximately a mile away and there was an urgency to their task. Supplies, especially of ammunition, were vital and resupply was already much needed. Added to this was an acute risk of coming under fire as the Germans were encroaching on the Allied positions and in some cases had overrun the dropping zones.

Unknown to the British, the locations of their supply dropping zones had been revealed to the Germans following the capture of a set of plans for Operation Market Garden from a downed glider. The prospect of danger was already disconcerting but the likelihood of something happening was now further increased. Still, it was vital to get food, ammunition and medical resupply forward to those British Airborne Battalions pressing to break through to the bridge at Arnhem to strengthen what hold the 2nd Parachute Battalion had on its northern end. First, however, they had to recover them. Crossing the railway bridge at Oosterbeek Holt, the drivers swung their jeeps rapidly onto the tree-lined Dreijenseweg road. Camouflaged and concealed among the foliage, a German tank was set in ambush. As the jeeps approached the tank opened fire with a thunderous blast and to lethal effect. The lead jeep was hit and the vehicles behind it piled into the back of each other. Dazed, the survivors helped their wounded comrades to escape the killing ground whilst Captain Kavanagh gave covering fire with a Bren gun. He maintained a supressing fire for long enough to allow the stumbling, staggering men of the Royal Army Service Corps to clear the scene. As the last man left the ambush site, 25-year-old Captain Desmond Kavanagh was killed. He is buried in the Airborne Cemetery at Oosterbeek.

It was also the day that Cork-born Flight Lieutenant David 'Lummy' Lord of 271 Squadron Transport Command RAF was killed in action when, despite his Dakota's starboard wing being on fire, he made not one, but two runs over the supply dropping zone to ensure that all his panniers of ammunition were despatched. Then he attempted to keep the stricken aircraft flying level for his crew to leave safely. Unfortunately, the damaged wing crumpled under pressure and the plane crashed. Nor was this the end to the tragedies which were to be heaped upon those attempting to get much-needed supplies to the Allied troops. On board Dakota call sign FZ-626 of 271 Squadron, which took off from Down Ampney airfield alongside Flight Lieutenant Lord heading for a supply dropping zone north of Oosterbeek, was Lance Corporal James Grace from Dublin. An Air Dispatcher with the Royal Army Service Corps, his was one of those aircraft hit by heavy ground fire as they came in over Arnhem. Struck several times by flak and sustaining severe damage, the dispatchers continued to push the panniers of supplies out of the Dakota as it maintained a steady level flight path over the designated supply dropping zone. Fatally hit and unable to fly any longer, the aircraft crashed onto a house and hit one of the German guns. The impact with the ground killed five of the eight-man crew, Lance Corporal Grace among them.

Most of the supplies that the gallant air crews were skilfully and courageously risking their lives to drop to the beleaguered troops below were in fact falling into the hands of the Germans, and the acute lack of supplies was beginning to become sharply felt by those engaged in the 1st British Airborne Division's attack. Their strength too was being steadily depleted as the Germans counter-attacked. Sergeant John Bermingham from Dublin, T Company 1st Parachute Battalion, was part of an early-morning attack eastward along the river road on the line of the Lower Rhine with the remainder of the 1 Parachute Brigade. Penetrating successfully to within 500 metres of the bridge, they paid an enormous price for their progress only to find themselves, once the morning fog lifted, facing the merciless crossfire of 20 mm anti-aircraft guns fired horizontally from across the river on the southern bank and from the German army blocking line north of them. Amongst the many to fall was Sergeant John Bermingham, who was one of three soldiers wounded near a factory complex. The three casualties were taken to the Casualty Clearing Station (CCS) at the St Elisabeth Hospital, where they were attended to by British medical staff, but Sergeant Bermingham died of his wounds and is buried in the Airborne Cemetery at Oosterbeek. Along with Sergeant Bermingham, Lieutenant Michael Kilmartin, Commander of No. 2 Platoon R Company 1st Parachute Battalion, from the Republic of Ireland, perished in the earlier fighting along the River road and is commemorated on the Groesbeck Memorial, having no known grave.

Taking and holding high ground has always been of importance to military men, and the high ground offered at Koepel was attractive to Brigadier John 'Shan' Hackett and his 4 Parachute Brigade, as it would greatly assist in his task of forming a defensive perimeter north of Arnhem. High ground bestows upon those holding it the advantage of clear sight lines and open fields of fire, and anyone attacking positions on high ground has the disadvantage of having to advance uphill in their attempt to do so. In short, high ground dominates and controls the surrounding terrain. Brigadier Hackett's father was originally from County Tipperary, a Trinity College graduate who had emigrated to Australia. John 'Shan' Hackett himself was commissioned into the 8th King's Royal Irish Hussars in 1933. His Parachute Brigade contained the 156th, 10th and 11th Parachute Battalions and they were tasked to take objectives at Koepel, on the Ede–Arnhem road and at Mariëndaal, respectively. All these attacks met with little success and proved costly in terms of manpower. It was here that Private Francis Dolaghan was killed and his brother Thomas, due to the ongoing fighting, had to leave his body where it lay as the 4 Brigade Headquarters continued its momentum.

Matters at the bridge itself were only slightly less serious, insofar as although the British managed to hold their positions, these were becoming much reduced in terms of both the buildings occupied and the numbers of troops, who were also greatly depleted. Lieutenant Reginald 'Danny Boy' Woods was badly wounded by shrapnel when the roof of the building he was in (known as the White House) collapsed after repeated shelling by a self-propelled anti-tank gun. When the men at Arnhem Bridge surrendered, the wounded Lieutenant Woods was carried to the railway station and sent to Stalag XI-B near Fallingbostel in north-western Germany, where he died of his wounds. All in all, the British at the bridge were barely holding on, had made no gains elsewhere, and had lost considerable numbers.

To further add to their woes, the Third Lift – that of the 1st Polish Parachute Regiment Brigade – was delayed due to bad weather and then only the glider-borne element departed. It successfully landed in the drop zone originally intended, but that area had not been secured, so the Germans played havoc with them on their arrival. By the end of the third day, many of the 1st British Airborne Division's Battalions were down to a third or less of the strength that had landed on 17 September. Resupply was not functioning properly, as the Germans had overrun the supply dropping zones, and the lack of radio communications meant the RAF could not be informed, so the reserve supply situation was critical. There were no reinforcements to speak of and the arrival of Horrocks' XXX Corps was nowhere in sight.

★★★

Some progress had been made on what was becoming known as 'Hell's Highway' because of the constantly contested nature of holding it open and trying to progress XXX Corps along it. The day began with the completion of the Bailey bridge at Son, allowing some movement across it but only as far as Nijmegen, where a struggle had developed for the bridge there. 'Jumping Jim' Gavin, Officer Commanding 82nd US Airborne Division, suggested a river crossing to assist in the simultaneous attack of both ends of the bridge at once. Only this meant assault boats had to be brought forward along the route through the congestion, involving more delays. Neither were the Germans idle; a number of attempts were made to cut the route at various points where the US Airborne were stretched a little thin on the ground. Antony Beevor mentions in *Arnhem* that on 19 September at Sint-Oedenrode, news reached Lieutenant Colonel Patrick Cassidy's 1st Battalion, 502nd Parachute Infantry Regiment, of the approach of German troops. Luckily, one of the Irish Guard's tanks from the Guards Armoured Division, which had passed through that morning, had experienced engine difficulties and remained behind to attempt repairs. Up against superior German forces supported by artillery, Lieutenant Colonel Cassidy requested the tank commander, Sergeant James 'Paddy' McCrory, a larger-than-life character, for support. Sergeant McCrory was happy to assist, albeit at a road speed of five miles per hour. With bullets flying around the tank's turret, he directed his Sherman down a track until he spotted a German flak battery of three 20 mm calibre guns. He ordered the gunner to put it out of action, and before the German artillery realised what was happening the battery was destroyed. The Sherman next encountered a concealed German anti-tank gun, which was identified and rendered useless, and shortly thereafter a German tank was engaged and blown up with an enormous explosion, suggesting it was full of munitions. As a result, a platoon of Germans was neutralised and twice as many made prisoner. Lieutenant Colonel Patrick Cassidy was to thank Sergeant Paddy McCrory personally; two Irishmen wearing different uniforms on foreign soil, bound in a moment of vigorous action to nullify the effect of Nazism.

The British 1st Airborne Division had experienced a mauling on Day Three and the situation only went from bad to worse as the day progressed. In the ebb and flow of the close-quarter fighting, various Battalion commanders were killed, wounded and captured, and the cohesion of the applied force was uncoordinated and its overall effort fragmented. It had one effect, however, that of drawing the German troops away from the area where Division Commander General Urquhart was hiding. Making his escape, he commandeered a jeep and soon reappeared at his Headquarters, to the surprise of those there who thought he had been killed or captured. Any solution to their situation lay in the now well overdue and, still unknown to them, overly delayed arrival of XXX Corps. But could they manage to hold out, even for one more day?

Food was scarce; the British Airborne Division had arrived with field rations enough for two days and were now facing a fourth. The Germans had turned off the water and electricity in areas occupied by the British, and they were largely keeping themselves armed by taking what ammunition they could from their dead and wounded comrades. If only XXX Corps could arrive in time, before the manpower, materials and morale deteriorated even further and they became completely exhausted. Not only were the British fighting an increasing number of Germans, but also against fatigue itself. They had expended most of their physical and mental energies and were coming close to the limits of their endurance; they were simply worn out. Over the last three days of continuous alertness, heightened tension and hard close-quarter fighting, they had maintained a determined, stoic defence at the northern end of the bridge, and although they were battered they were proving difficult to dislodge. Simultaneously, the British were keeping up the pressure of attempted advances through the suburbs into the town, to reach the bridge and reinforce the troops there. Concurrently, other elements of the British Airborne Division were fighting to keep the landing and drop zones open and secure. All the while they were outgunned by an enemy growing stronger by the day. Fewer British Airborne troops had to endure increasing firepower that the ever-arriving Germans inflicted upon them.

By Day Three Arnhem had become an intensely scary place: a tough, frightening and dangerous battle space. There was a lot of gunfire, killing and dying, none of it seemly, some of it horrible. Incremental increases in the pressure being applied by the German Army would eventually bring about a 'tipping point' in the situation on the ground; the question was, had it arrived already or would it arrive before XXX Corps? The expectancy of the arrival of XXX Corps continued to instil in the British at Arnhem enough hope that was strong enough to sustain them; the emotive power of a dearly-held belief that kept them going physically and psychologically. Yet the pressure could still tip them beyond their current state of exhaustion, or the physical circumstance that the Germans might impose would mean their mental resolve would run out, as it eventually must. Indeed, would any of them be alive by then?

6

INSIDE THE PERIMETER (20 SEPTEMBER 1944)

'Charge!' came the shout, and as one 150 British Airborne troops with bayonets fixed emerged over the rim of the large natural crater in which they were sheltering. Yelling, roaring and bawling, they ran straight towards their disbelieving German attackers in a scene more reminiscent of an 'over the top' bayonet charge from the trench warfare of the Great War some twenty-five years previously. It was all the more remarkable because it worked. Officer Commanding 4 Parachute Brigade, Brigadier General John 'Shan' Hackett, the son of an immigrant Australian father from Tipperary, and his men had found themselves in a near hopeless situation, and he led the desperate manoeuvre in a bid to break the deadlock. Breaking cover and running bare-headed directly at the enemy troops over distance was unmistakably unorthodox, but it succeeded in unnerving and catching their attackers' off-balance.

The dire circumstances of their predicament demanded the British Airborne troops attempt this unthinkable dash for freedom. Taking the old adage, 'when all else fails proceed with full confidence' to an extreme, it was a case of desperate times calling for desperate measures. With weapons blazing, Sten guns and rifles pouring out their last precious rounds they made their seemingly suicidal breakout, yelling, screaming and charging at the astonished Germans. So shocked were the German troops, they scattered and the paratroopers kept on running until they reached the safety of the 1st British Airborne Division Perimeter at Oosterbeek, centred around the Hartenstein Hotel.

Ordered into the newly created perimeter, the 4th Parachute Brigade had moved from the south east of Wolfheze and were advancing through woodlands towards Oosterbeek when they ran into a major enemy force and came under concentrated machine-gun, mortar and self-propelled gunfire. Seeking safety in a sunken hollow in the tree-lined terrain, which provided some sanctuary from the bullets and shrapnel of the ferocious machine-gun strafing and flak gunfire that was raining down on them, they quickly found that any attempt to outmanoeuvre their attackers or undertake any flanking movement only seemed to further exacerbate their predicament. As German tanks were encountered and casualties mounted, small groups were isolated and captured, and entire companies of the 10th and 156 Parachute Battalions became separated. Fortuitously, finding and establishing a defence within the sunken trough amongst the trees, C Company of 156 Parachute Battalion were joined by 4 Parachute Brigade Headquarters personnel.

This group of approximately 150 paratroopers were rallied by Brigadier John 'Shan' Hackett and readied into a defence, which they conducted for the remainder of the day, sustaining many fatalities and wounded. Nevertheless, they managed to hold off constant attempts by the enemy to overrun their position. This hastily assembled defence held well for several hours, but with increasing pressure from the enemy in the surrounding woods, and with ammunition running low, there came a gradual realisation that should matters continue in this vein the inevitable outcome was certain death or capture. Brigadier Hackett decided to drastically change the dynamic before this inescapable outcome came to pass, and with one wild, reckless roll of the dice they rose up and routed the enemy in their path, clearing a way through to the safety of the perimeter not far off. The naturally occurring undulation in the woods from which they sprang was thereafter known as 'Hackett's Hollow'.

The previous day, the four battalions (the 1st, 3rd and 11th Parachute Battalions and the 2nd Battalion of the South Staffordshire's Airlanding

Brigade) whose advance through the town to the bridge proved unsuccessful, also tragically saw them decimated in numbers to the extent that they ceased to exist as viable individual units. At the same time, newly liberated from his enforced confinement in the attic of a local Dutch family's house, the Airborne Division Commander, General Urquhart's attempt to use Hackett's 4 Parachute Brigade and Hicks's Airlanding Brigade to shape the Arnhem Battle space within which they fought towards a more favourable outcome, proved equally unsuccessful.

The way to the bridge firmly blocked, a badly battered and much depleted 2nd Parachute Battalion barely held on, despite fighting like demons. Their capacity to continue already overstretched, they could not possibly be expected to last much longer; the Germans were in control of the town and, with constantly arriving reinforcements, were exerting ever mounting pressure. So how could the British maintain the initiative? It was already a tight contest and had seen some key moments, but with all that had happened it was difficult to see how they could grind out a victory. If cohesion in attack was not achieved, perhaps composure in defence might bring results. Although they could not gain ground, maybe they could win by not losing it; unable to change their point of attack, could they change their point of defence? By assembling the remnants of his Division into a thumb-shaped pocket at Oosterbeek, with its base on the Lower Rhine specifically encompassing the area of the currently out of action Heveadorp ferry, Urquhart planned to form a bridgehead on the northern bank of the river and bring the ferry back into working order. The idea being the redirected 1st Polish Parachute Brigade would now be landed at Driel to secure the southern bank.

As Hackett had done in the Hollow, Urquhart hoped to repeat at Oosterbeek and he formed a defensive perimeter, in the centre of which was his divisional headquarters at the Hartenstein Hotel. With the arrival of the remaining elements of Hackett's 4 Parachute Brigade,

Major General Urquhart divided the defensive perimeter into eastern and western sectors commanded by Brigadier Generals Hackett and Hicks respectively. The northern arching bow of the curved top of the perimeter was the responsibility of the 21st Independent Parachute Company and the 7th Battalion, The King's Own Scottish Borders. The eastern side was defended by the residue of the 10th and 156 Parachute Battalions with men from the Glider Pilot Regiment and 1st Airlanding Light Regiment, Royal Artillery, while the western side was defended by the 1st Battalion, the Border Regiment and a jumbled concoction of engineers, glider pilots and Polish troops who had arrived and survived the glider drop of the Polish 1st Independent Parachute Brigade's anti-tank guns – and a mishmash of men from several other units. The southern end of the perimeter was the responsibility of the 'Lonsdale Force', a conglomeration of the remains of the 1st, 3rd and 11th Parachute Battalions, together with the 7th Battalion, The South Staffordshire Regiment, and the gun line (75 mm Howitzers) of the Light Regiment, Royal Artillery, which was near Oosterbeek church.

The 'Lonsdale Force' was a 'cobbled together' unit of paratroopers and airborne South Staffs under Major Richard 'Dickie' Lonsdale, second in command of the 11th Parachute Battalion. The youngest son of Mr and Mrs Robert Lonsdale of Lancefield, Camberley, and Carrick-on-Shannon, County Leitrim, he is believed born in Manorhamilton, County Leitrim and was raised in England. He won the Military Cross in Wazirisitan in August 1936 with the 1st Battalion Leicester Regiment (later the Royal Leicestershire) and the Distinguished Service Order in Sicily in 1943 as Commander of A Company 2nd Parachute Battalion. He had been wounded in the hand by flak shrapnel just before jumping at Arnhem and was hit twice more, so his appearance – swathed in bloodied bandages – was somewhat fearsome.

Lieutenant Colonel W.F.K. 'Sheriff' Thompson, 1st Airlanding Light Regiment Royal Artillery (1st Airborne Division's Own Artillery) had provided 'fire missions' (fire support) for the brigades and battalions since their arrival at Arnhem, but became concerned that as the situation evolved there was now no protective screen of troops in front of his guns and he gathered up retreating paratroopers from their failed advance towards the bridge. This was initially referred to as 'Thompson's Force' and was the nucleus for what shortly thereafter became designated as the 'Lonsdale Force' once 'Dickie' Lonsdale was assigned to take command of them. Major Lonsdale set up his headquarters near Oosterbeek church and was renowned for his energetic encouragement of those around him. On one famous occasion, he ordered his exhausted men into Oosterbeek church and appeared in the pulpit with one arm in a bloodstained sling, a bandaged leg and a further bloodstained bandage wrapped around his head. He addressed them stirringly with the words: 'You know as well as I do there are a lot of bloody Germans coming at us. We've fought the Germans before ... They were not good enough for us then and they are bloody well not good enough for us now. They're up against the finest soldiers in the world!'

The 'ring of steel' now placed around the encircled British Oosterbeek perimeter, about four miles distant from the bridge, set in motion another phase of the battle. With constant German sniping and mortar barrages, these were compounded by intermittent infantry and tank attacks. With the fight for the bridge and their hopes of success ebbing away by the hour, the British at the Oosterbeek perimeter were desperately fighting for time. All the while casualties mounted, and among those killed in action were Lance Corporal Patrick Harrington from Durrus, County Cork, 11th Parachute Battalion; Private William Patrick Devlin, the Hong Kong born son of an Irish soldier, 9 Platoon, T Company, 1st Parachute Battalion; Major James Ivor 'Happy' Houston from Derry, Headquarter Company, 3rd Parachute Battalion; and Sergeant John Hunter from County Antrim, Platoon Sergeant of 10 Platoon A Company, 1st Parachute Battalion. Others from Ireland, North and South, were wounded and captured.

★★★

A Situation Report to the effect that 'Relief was urgently requested' was received by General 'Boy' Browning around midday on 20 September.

Finally, after four days an awareness and understanding of the dire straits that the British at Arnhem were in was in his hands. Meanwhile, the stubborn stand by Lieutenant Colonel Frost's 2nd Parachute Battalion continued; he had been wounded in both legs by a mortar blast and joined the many wounded filling the cellars below the houses left in contention. His second-in-command, Major Freddie Gough, was one of a long line of famous Irish soldiers; he had served in the Royal Navy during the Great (First World) War and was back in action for the Second World War. For his bravery in Italy he had been awarded the Military Cross and at Arnhem he was Commander 1st Airborne Reconnaissance Squadron. Major Gough had managed to reach the bridge with three of his jeeps in the late evening of the first day of Operation Market Garden and employed his Vickers mounted K-Type machine-guns to good effect ever since. Now it was a case of '2 I/C take over' (Second-in-Command take over command) something every second-in-command must be prepared for, and he was.

On the other hand, unprepared for his untimely death on 20 September was 29-year-old Lance Corporal Daniel Neville from Listowel, County Kerry, 1st Parachute Squadron Royal Engineers. Fighting alongside his fellow sappers in the school building, he was killed when German tanks and self-propelled guns approaching from the town side of the bridge came to within 100 metres and from there stood off and blasted the building. Quickly catching fire, the structure began to collapse and the wounded were evacuated while those not wounded attempted to make a fighting escape through the streets. Lance Corporal Neville was killed during the evacuation. Barely holding on, their dogged defiance to give up what the British had now come to regard as 'their' bridge had the significant effect of denying the German SS Panzer Corps (9th and 10th SS Panzer Divisions) access to the bridge and onto Nijmegen. Crossing the bridge would have allowed the German armour to contribute to resisting the advance of the Guards Armoured Division towards Arnhem once they had secured the river crossing there.

The road bridge north of Nijmegen was captured undamaged after a valiant river crossing by the US 82nd Airborne Division shortly after 1900 hours and XXX Corps' leading armoured column moved swiftly across it. They were 10 miles (17 km) from Arnhem, and for the depleted British Airborne Division at Arnhem, their long awaited and much delayed arrival up the last section of 'Hell's Highway' would be heaven sent. But in the shifting and uncertain circumstances, in the midst of the chaos of trying to protect their tactical position they had to concentrate on a new crisis. They were very few now, and those left were struggling to hold on to the northern approaches to the Arnhem road bridge. Divisional Headquarters at the Hartenstein Hotel in the Oosterbeek perimeter had no contact with them and could neither reinforce nor resupply them. The whole of Arnhem was in enemy hands, and even Dubliner Lance Corporal Mick Cox and his section of 'Red Caps', 1st Airborne Provost Company (Military Police) had come to the notice of the Germans, who launched an assault on their occupation of the Arnhem Police Station with intense machine-gun fire and the liberal use of hand grenades. Sergeant Calloway was killed and the remainder taken prisoner, Mick Cox amongst them, though three of the 'occupants' managed to escape. Relief for the situation at Arnhem was urgently requested and desperately needed. A fierce battle was now raging around the Arnhem road bridge and the Oosterbeek perimeter, and the enemy were attacking both with grit and determination. The outlook was serious, though a panorama of the battle at this point in time would reveal that with the Nijmegen bridge secure and the Guards Armoured Division streaming across it, the road ahead to Arnhem was lightly defended. It was an imaginable scenario where despite everything victory for the Allies was a distinct possibility, only incredulously, the Armoured Division stopped! Lack of infantry support may have contributed to this. Exasperatingly close to victory, caution won out over courage; giving truth to the old adage, 'Leadership cannot be taught; it must be learned.'

7

DER HEXENKESSEL (THE WITCHES' CAULDRON) (21 SEPTEMBER 1944)

Surrounded, and battered, the British Airborne troops were under constant machine-gun and mortar bombardment. The British suffered many wounded, dead and dying, but still refused to surrender the perimeter at Oosterbeek. The German attacks were relentless, there were mortar bombs impacting around and on their positions, artillery shells exploding and tracer bullets whizzing overhead. The noise was overwhelming, the situation was perilous and their position precarious as ammunition, food and water ran low. Nerves were frayed and the tension only increased as the noose tightened. They did not know when or if they would be reinforced or rescued, and if actually resupplied they did not know if they could hold out. The 'Perimeter' defenders were bruised, but not broken.

Then, ominously amid the rumpus, through the rubble could be heard the distinct and unmistakeable creaking and clattering of tank tracks. Already encircled and endangered, the British Airborne now had to prepare for a tank assault. The orders went out: 'PIAT, PIAT, bring forward the PIAT!' An equal measure of despair and defiance was detectable in the voice, but urgency was uppermost for sure. The PIAT, the 'Projector, Infantry, Anti-Tank' was a British-made, hand-held portable anti-tank weapon that was heavy to carry, awkward to use and cumbersome to fire (difficult to cock and it had a powerful recoil), though it was very reassuring to have available. With a reliable range of over 100-metres it ranked as outstandingly effective in the hands of paratroopers and others prepared to use it properly. One such pair of hands belonged to Major Robert Cain of the South Staffordshire Regiment, and having used the PIAT to good effect over the preceding few days he took up the challenge once more and stealthily went in pursuit of a good firing position. Joining him in the stalking of the 'Tiger' tank was Sergeant John Daly from County Waterford, 1st Airlanding Light Regiment, Royal Artillery, to provide covering fire with a Bren gun (a light machine-gun). A Tiger tank is a formidable fighting vehicle to confront, and if one is at all prone towards movement when one appears, the impulse is definitely away from it, not forwards. It is better to seek cover or flight, not go head on and fight what was reported to have been a Tiger tank.

It is, however, within the remit of human conduct for tenacity to win out over terror; fatalism over fear; control over faintheartedness. To feel fear and master it is true courage and in battle this behaviour can lead to belligerence, as was displayed by Major Cain and Sergeant Daly. Infantry support is used in combination with armour to prevent against the type of attack that Cain and Daly intended to effect. Along with the creaking of the tank tracks as the Tiger drew nearer, discernible too was the rumble of its sheer mass. Walls vibrated as the tank's weight and bulk caused the ground around it to tremble and already damaged structures to shake precariously. On it advanced, in a manner that exuded menace, an inherent jeopardy evident in its confrontation as the Tiger sought prey to destroy.

Unaware that the hunter was itself being hunted, the Tiger advanced. Allowed to come closer, all the better to bring it well within effective firing range, the surer were the waiting British soldiers of 'the kill'. As the moment of engagement edged closer the suspense of uncertainty mounted, but Major Cain kept a check on his impulse to act prematurely and patiently waited and judged when it was the optimum moment to fire. It was nearing, but not just yet … hold on, hold on. And then it was in perfect position. He fired the PIAT and the 2.5 pound (1.1 kg) shaped charge struck the Tiger tank. There was a huge impact explosion, the smoke and flames momentarily hiding the tank from the view of its attackers. When the smoke cleared they could see that the tank was immobilised but its gun was still operable. Sergeant Daly set up covering fire to keep the accompanying German infantry and the machine gunners inside the tank from attacking their position. This barrage of voluminous, accurate and sustained firing allowed Major Cain the time to reload, take aim and loose off another PIAT bomb, resulting in a second and decisive hit. With the Tiger tank out of action the discouraged German infantry withdrew, those who were too slow cut down by other British paratroopers who joined in the now equal firefight. The threat was over for now, but there were other Tiger tanks, Panzers and Mark IVs out there and there were other hits against them. Major Cain was later awarded the Victoria Cross for his action (the only such award during the battle that was not posthumous) and Sergeant Daly was awarded the Distinguished Conduct Medal.

On the fifth day, the course of the battle swung away from the defenders at the bridge. The situation there had already gone from serious to critical and was becoming overwhelming. They could hold out no longer and were overrun. Victory was beyond them, but it was their ammunition which became expended, not their courage. The wounded were taken prisoner, Lieutenant Reginald 'Danny Boy' Woods among them. Transferred by train to prisoner-of-war camp Stalag XI-B, he was to die of his wounds and is buried in Becklingen Cemetery. Those that could made an attempt to infiltrate the perimeter, but not all made it through German lines and most were killed, captured or wounded. Some hid amongst the rubble and burned-out buildings hoping to evade capture – few were successful.

With the bridge at Arnhem now open to the Germans, the dynamic of the battle – already characterised by constant change and activity, both energetic and forceful – was altered yet again. SS-Obergruppenführer Wilhelm Bittrich could now advance his east and west blocking lines inwards in unison to crush the perimeter. He was not content to simply defeat the British, rather he wanted to destroy them. For Bittrich this final phase of the battle was not going to be one of attrition, rather it was to be one of annihilation. The second major consequence of the road bridge at Arnhem falling into German hands was that their movement towards Nijmegen was no longer hindered. They were now better enabled to obstruct the Allied advance towards Arnhem by pouring reinforcements and armour towards Elst, preventing XXX Corps reaching Arnhem by breaking their approach.

Yet a further variation came into play with the arrival of General Stanisław Sosabowski and the Polish 1st Independent Parachute Brigade, not at their original drop zone but instead at Driel near the ferry terminal area, so that his force could be ferried across the Rhine from the southern bank to relieve the 'Red Devils' (1st Parachute Division). He was unaware that the actual Heveadorp ferry had not been located. An unintended consequence of the arrival of the Polish Parachute Brigade was its misinterpretation by the Germans as a new initiative by the Allies to block German movement southwards, indeed another audacious attempt to seize the Arnhem road bridge from the southern end, and not an attempt to reinforce the 1st Airborne Division at Oosterbeek. In order to deal with this risk, a large force of Germans were redirected from pressuring the Oosterbeek perimeter to instead secure the route south forward of the bridge, thereby placing a significant blocking force between it and XXX Corps and sealing the last chance of success for Operation Market Garden's prize objective, the successful link up to secure a river crossing at Arnhem. Unwittingly, just maybe the Polish paratroopers could still affect the outcome.

With Dunkirk remaining in German hands, they had observed the progress of the Polish Parachute Brigade overhead at approximately 1600 hours (4 pm) as they crossed the French coast. Their reports alerted the German flak batteries on the route of the Allied flight path and also gave sufficient warning to allow the Luftwaffe put 100 fighter aircraft into the skies. Escorting Allied Typhoon fighter-bombers substantially addressed the anti-aircraft threat and other escorting fighters were a match for the would-be German air interception. Inevitably, some Dakotas were downed (thirteen) and a far larger group (some thirty-five Dakotas) were forced to turn back because of bad weather. Those who did make it to Driel arrived

66

to a landing and drop zone raked by German machine-gun and mortar fire. In all, fewer than 1,000 Polish paratroopers put their feet on Dutch soil, casualties amongst them. All the while, the Irish were at the forefront. One amongst the Poles who fought at Driel was Sergeant Eric Matson from Bandon, County Cork, Glider Pilot Regiment. A co-pilot in a Hamilcar glider, he managed to land his aircraft intact, unlike the previous day when Flight Sergeant Andrew Murphy was killed while on a resupply flight to Arnhem. His Stirling aircraft (LJ-988) flying from Keevil airfield, crashed at Natuurbad Doorwerth, west of Oosterbeek, and there were no survivors.

With the distraction caused by the arrival of the Poles, the contest north of the river was experiencing a slight ease, though this of little consolation and consequence to Private Patrick Sullivan from County Wicklow, 11th Parachute Battalion, who was killed in action west of the Hartenstein Hotel. There was an ebb and flow in the battle as ground was gained and lost, regained and held, so that the 'Perimeter' was not a well-defined forward edge of battle area, but instead a messy, contested, ill-defined one. Among the ground lost was a steep hill at Westerbouwing, overlooking the Rhine and the ferry crossing at the south western part of the perimeter. It was an important gain for the Germans, and with the perimeter contracting most of its southern side was in German hands, the British troops at the base of the perimeter retreating and losing more men.

The exertion of the fighting, the struggle to stay alive, and the effort to remain alert were all exhausting. The danger, the fear, and the drama all had its adverse effect; add to this the fact that sleep was impossible and the cumulative effect was debilitating and draining. There was an evident strain and people coped with it in their own way. The first four days over, the uncertainty of events had continued into a fifth. Shock was beginning to manifest in some troops and this in turn came as a shock to others. Not everything can be explained by logic; why some paratroopers could deal with the mental and emotional distress of the pressure, tension and confusion of the circumstances they faced in Arnhem whilst others beside them struggled but coped and others still became overwhelmed was anyone's guess. The exposure to danger and death was unsettling, the uncertainty and anxiety no less reassuring. The suddenness, intensity and duration of those extreme events caused vulnerability to become apparent. Those noticeably impacted by close firing, near misses and other abnormal stressors of battle were removed from the front line to the perimeter's interior to avoid additional strain being placed upon them before they became further dazed, disorientated and ultimately dysfunctional.

That night remained relatively quiet, before it all began again the next day.

8

BLACK FRIDAY
(22 SEPTEMBER 1944)

The sharp staccato sound of rounds being fired, bullet ricochets and the rattle of machine-guns rang around the Oosterbeek perimeter. Added to this the 'crump' of mortars, the 'thump' of artillery and the signature banshee wail of the six-barrelled 'Moaning Minnie' formed a never-ending cacophony which offered little respite to the defending Airborne troops. Raw and raucous, a battle is an angry place to be. Fiery muzzle flashes, the arching, stark brilliance of tracer trajectory, and vividly coloured impacts against walls and into cobbled roadways were dazzling, dramatic and dangerous. There was almost a magnificence, a splendid surrealism and an insane intensity to it all and the sights, sounds and sensations of the frenzied German attack and the frantic British Airborne defence assaulted the senses. This was a new stage in the week-long fight in the reshaped Arnhem battle space.

In the midst of all this turmoil, disturbance and confusion was Major Tony Blake, born in County Wicklow, Brigade Major with the 1st Airlanding Brigade Headquarters. Embattled and exhausted, he had faced adversity almost from the very start of Operation Market Garden. On 19 September, four officers of the 1st Airlanding Brigade Headquarters were killed by a German mortar shell in the Arnhem area, with Major Blake temporarily blinded by the same shell. He refused to go for treatment and remained at the field telephone and radios in a slit trench. His sight did not fully return until after evacuation, but until then he was constantly on duty throughout this period of intense mortar and artillery fire. With XXX Corps now in close proximity to Arnhem, Major Blake was fortuitously able to establish communications with them via a shared radio frequency, and this enabled him to direct the artillery fire of 64 Medium Regiment who were supporting the 1st Airborne Division from ten miles away. He carried out the direction of artillery fire quietly and efficiently, and their highly accurate 'fall of shot' broke up enemy concentrations and attacks and drastically decreased the German advantage. Without this artillery support fire the Oosterbeek perimeter could not have held.

With this added firepower support, the Airborne resistance stiffened. Thoroughly shaken, and with his sight greatly impaired, Major Blake displayed the greatest courage and determination throughout the operation in carrying out his duties cheerfully and most efficiently. He was awarded the US Distinguished Service Cross, gazetted on 14 November 1947. Major Tony Blake's medal display was recently exhibited at the award-winning *Soldiers & Chiefs* exhibition at the National Museum of Ireland, Collins Barracks, Dublin. A pre-war soldier, post-Sandhurst he was commissioned into the Royal Ulster Rifles in 1931, subsequently serving with the 1st Battalion in Egypt, Hong Kong, Shanghai and India. In 1938, he went to Russia on a course and was completing it in Warsaw when the Germans attacked Poland. He escaped, making his way back via Romania. He was to hold a number of training and staff appointments, including as an Intelligence Officer in the War Office and the Middle East. He also served in the Russia Liaison Group. At the end of Operation Market Garden he was among those to escape across the Rhine at the end of the battle. He remained in the army after the war and was killed in action in Korea in early January 1951.

A 'perimeter defence' can be a structured, deliberate line of defence, organised to give depth with a mutually supporting series of strong points with interlocking arches of fire and forward defensive screens. Even a hastily put together all-round defensive position and situation can adapt its circumstances to informally incorporate the principles employed in an otherwise more established and considered defence. The strong points are often referred to as hedgehogs, because even within the perimeter's protection they are designed to be standalone, three-hundred-and-sixty degree (360°) self-protecting positions, so if the area within the perimeter is overrun they can of themselves hold out until the ground around them is retaken by the defenders. Another feature of a perimeter defence is in line with other types of defences, in that it is not necessarily static or 'passive'; it can be active in that between major moments of countering concentrated attacks it sends out 'fighting' patrols.

Rarely fixed, a perimeter's defensive line can be fluid and fluctuate as the action around it – of enemy offensive assaults and defenders' defensive efforts – swing and seesaw with positions held, lost and retaken. The line may be penetrated here and pushed back there, and it may not necessarily have been neatly linear to begin with. With German patrols probing the perimeter looking for weak spots, British Airborne patrols sought to neutralise German snipers. Any part of the perimeter, even if it was not being attacked, could see activity along it, and patrols pursued their designated tasks as ordered. The boundaries between specified areas of responsibility are particularly vulnerable, as individual units may leave these areas for others to defend and it might end up being ignored and undefended; or gaps might occur due to deaths and destruction, particularly after an engagement.

It is advisable to confirm the integrity of the line to ensure that one's own troops and those of one's neighbouring units are intact and capable of continuing a defensive effort. Sent out to do just that, a four-man patrol from the 21st Independent Parachute Company (Pathfinders) ventured out from their position at Pietersbergseweg towards Annastraat where the 10th Parachute Battalion were *in situ*. Proceeding down lanes, through back gardens and over obstacles, Private Tommy Scullion from County Antrim laid down necessary covering fire with his Bren gun as Private James Vincent Fiely from Dublin, another Irishman in the patrol, and the others moved forward. On arrival at their objective, the patrol occupied a house along the perimeter and noticed the presence of troops in an adjacent building. Enquiring of their unknown neighbours if they were from the 10th Parachute Battalion, their query was answered in the form of an abrupt eruption of gunfire as the German occupiers opened up with machine-guns and grenades. Private Fiely, in a kneeling position at the exterior corner of the house, was mowed down and died immediately. A firefight developed and the remaining three Pathfinders managed to extricate themselves from their situation. The danger of their position had been monitored by other Pathfinders in a house further down the street (who were aware of the German presence but were unable to warn the patrol in time), who offered support fire from their position, distracting the attention of the Germans and allowing the patrol to make good their escape. Out of necessity they had to leave the body of Private Fiely behind. Also killed in action on 22 September was Private Patrick 'Paddy' Hurley from the Republic, serving with the 1st Battalion Border Regiment.

Concurrent activities were ongoing all day along the perimeter as the battle raged, with an attack here, a concentration of mortar fire there, patrols fighting elsewhere and of course within the perimeter there were those fighting to save the lives of the critically and seriously wounded. Three buildings at the Oosterbeek crossroads, the Schoonoord, the Tafeberg and the Vreewijk hotels, were converted into temporary dressing stations during the battle, with doctors and medical orderlies from the Royal Army Medical Corps doing their best in desperate conditions to render medical aid as well as they could in the circumstances. Military Chaplains and local padres gave spiritual comfort where appropriate, their services unfortunately all too frequently required. The men of the 1st Airborne Division were doing two things at the same time: fighting their German attackers and waiting for the arrival of XXX Corps. They were all too aware that their situation was not ideal, but they were optimistic about what they believed was the imminent arrival of XXX Corps to relieve them and they were determined to hold out until reinforcements arrived. In the interim, the continued non-arrival of the resupply drops was a source of constant frustration.

It was not the fault of the RAF, indeed their courage and sacrifice were admirable, but the supplies were falling in the wrong places. Correctly speaking, they were landing in the 'right' locations, but the British on the ground no longer held these positions and communicating this fact had not been a success; so the valiant efforts of the RAF were largely in vain. Various estimates of the resupply received fluctuate between 7 and 13 per cent of what was actually dropped, so an approximate average of 10 per cent is a good working guide to go on and accurately illustrates their plight. To fight they needed ammunition, and to wait they needed to stay alive. They also desperately needed food, water and rest. Of course, they also had to avoid being killed, and German snipers and mortars were constantly doing their utmost to achieve that!

Mortar fire is deadly, its lethality derived not so much from the explosive effect, unless it was an unlikely but possible direct hit, but rather from the slivers of shrapnel produced from the shredding of the outer metallic case of the mortar charge on impact; a typical mortar bomb has a killing radius of 25–50 metres. The larger the calibre, the greater the killing area. Mortar bombs are launched upwards and towards the target in an indirect trajectory following an arch, rather than in a straight line onto a target area. Mortars themselves are little more than metal tubes with a fixed firing pin at the bottom. The desired direction and distance of the target is governed by the angle and elevation at which it is set, thereby controlling the fall of shot. The mortar bomb, or round, is dropped down the tube and the firing pin strikes a cartridge in the base of the bomb which ignites propellant and projects it skywards. Tail fins fitted to the base of the bomb keep its flight steady and true towards the target. Mortar bombs are packed with high explosives that fragment on impact and individual pinpoint precision is not required due to the dispersive nature of the deadly shrapnel.

Accuracy, especially over distance, can be hampered by poor use of the weapon, varying wind direction or fluctuating wind strengths, and can cause mortar bombs to fall short, go further than intended or go wide of the target. Some may fall on or near the target area but do not explode, and personnel need to be wary of these 'blinds' because they could still explode by themselves or if inadvertently disturbed. There is also a potential danger that in a rapid fire situation a mortar bomb may be dropped down the tube but does not launch, only for the mortar crew – thinking that the previous round has exited – to drop a subsequent mortar bomb down the tube, which immediately explodes on contact with the one already there; this is known as a 'double feed' and can result in the death or wounding of a mortar team and those around them.

The mortar's main use, as an indirect fire support weapon, is to suppress enemy movement in defence or attack, to subdue their activities and to keep any advance in check. Mortars are also used to lay down defensive fire or to otherwise 'fix' an opponent in position whilst one's own troops manoeuvre in the advance. Fired singularly, in pairs, or in groups, the more mortar bombs arriving onto a position, the more ground surface is covered, and in this sense it is an 'area' weapon. Such a grouping of mortars are referred to as a battery and their fire as mortar battery fire. Their use at Arnhem was not the sole preserve of any one side, often mortar fire was used to respond to that of the opposition's mortar fire, and such counter-battery (CB) fire was conducted by mortars of equal calibre. These duels frequently escalated in the numbers of mortars employed and the addition of artillery: German 88s or Allied Airborne howitzers (75 mm). Because they are fired indirectly and are concealed from each other's observers, a mortar-fire controller (MFC) or 'spotter' (for the artillery it is a Forward Observation Officer, FOO) gives directions and adjustments of the fall of shot onto the target. Like Major Tony Blake, for the spotter to operate effectively they must have direct line of sight onto the target to see the round's impact, how near, far or wide it was, and to communicate with the mortar or artillery firing line to call in adjustments. Discovering each other's spotters' position – 'spotting the spotter' – and neutralising them is an effective means of disrupting mortar fire and this makes the job a hazardous one. Far more hazardous, of course, is to be under a mortar barrage.

The best defence is to put distance between yourself and that area as quickly as possible using the best cover available. If you cannot remove yourself but are duty-bound to remain where you are, then to make yourself safe you quite literally have to occupy the ground that you must hold by digging into it. As the name implies, 'slit trenches' and firing positions can be excavated from the earth, with overhead protection built in, to retreat into and take cover from mortar and artillery barrages. All defensive trenches are camouflaged and strict occupation discipline is imposed. Depth is added to the defensive position by the siting of trenches over distance rearwards, to prevent the position from being easily overrun. Support weapon trenches should be sited tactically, bearing in mind the nature of the terrain, and well dug in troops can be difficult to dislodge. Given that the perimeter consisted of a mixture of built-up suburban, open ground and woodland-type terrain, there were prepared defences in variations of slit trenches in gardens, streets and residential houses and buildings, which were fortified to different degrees. What remained of the 1st Airborne Division occupied a combination of these 'protection from fire' positions, from where they would do their fighting and waiting.

The first major challenge had come early the previous day when the Germans made their first moves to eliminate the Airborne pocket. They actually succeeded in driving the 1st Battalion Border Regiment off the Westerbouwing Heights, a 30-metre stretch of high ground overlooking the Heveadorp ferry, and pushed them back some 800 metres in all. With the western and eastern sides of the perimeter already contained by blocking lines, now a third, a southern one, was almost fully in position. The Germans were creating a box around the perimeter, and it only remained for them to put a lid on the northern side. What was left of the Borders concentrated around a large white house in Dennenoord. Those Airborne defenders on the northern tip of the perimeter, the 7th King's Own Scottish Borderers (KOSB), had a 'white house' of their own to defend, the Dreijerood Hotel.

When first called upon to defend the hotel, they had been subjected to an intense, creeping mortar barrage behind which troops from Kampfgruppe Krafft advanced. When the mortar barrage lifted to allow the attacking Germans to conduct their crossing of the final assault line, the defenders emerged from their prepared covered positions, took up firing positions and opened up with everything they had. Riflemen, Bren gunners, Vickers machine gunners, mortar crews with mortar elevations almost directly vertical laid down a sustained and effective combined fire. The unfaltering barrage began to have its effect and the German attack stuttered, stalled a little, then completely stopped and they broke in disarray, retreating backwards. Others went to ground and were cleared with a bayonet charge. Not yet in sufficient force to inflict the fury and havoc they wished, the Germans settled in for a sustained imposition of constant harassing sniper and mortar fire for the remainder of that day.

Meanwhile, along Hell's Highway the route was living up to its name. Those on whom the remnants of the British 1st Airborne Division were relying witnessed a determined German pincer attack at Veghel, a choke point identified as vulnerable by General Kurt Student, who sent Kampfgruppe Huber from the west and Kampfgruppe Walther from the east to cut the route, split the Allied convoy's advance and impede their progress. Lieutenant General Brian Horrocks had to get the 32nd Guards (Infantry) Brigade to do an about turn and drive south to bring relief to the besieged defenders. Concurrently, renewed attempts by XXX Corps to force open the German defences on the route north of Nijmegen to Arnhem at Elst were proving unsuccessful. The Poles at Driel, whose overnight attempt to ferry reinforcements across the Rhine to Heveadorp resulted in only some fifty or so successfully reaching the far side, had to fight to hold open the corridor. From the concentration of effort to force the door open just short of Arnhem, the Poles slightly west of Arnhem proved no less successful in reaching the other side. All gave their utmost, but the setbacks led to Lieutenant General Horrocks naming Friday 22 September 'Black Friday'. If he had known that II SS Panzer Corps Commander SS-Obergruppenführer Wilhelm Bittrich was conferring with Obersturmbannführer Walter Harzer of the 9th SS-Panzer Division 'Hohenstaufen' and Generalleutnant Hans von Tettau, to plan the final destruction of the Airborne troops in the perimeter – 'to put the lid on the box' – the very next day, 23 September, he might have called it something worse.

9

UNDER BOMBARDMENT (23 SEPTEMBER 1944)

Pounded ceaselessly and without mercy, the German bombardment of the Oosterbeek perimeter reportedly included some of the most murderous concentrated barrages of the two World Wars. Defending from foxholes, slit trenches, weapon pits, bomb craters and fortified houses, the men of the 1st Airborne Division withstood a punitive and punishing shelling. The Germans, conventional in siege-style warfare, were looking to first break and then penetrate the perimeter. Tactically, by maintaining a defence and simply continuing to exist the Airborne Division were winning. Enduring encroachment by infantry and tanks and assailment by artillery, they kept the German attackers and defeat at bay. It was by any measure an unequal fight, however they continued to hold out and stifled the impact of the German blitzkrieg.

The training of the Airborne troops had nurtured and developed within them resilience, vibrancy, confidence and cohesion. This collective energy, when collaboratively turned on, generated a remarkable defiance. Inevitably, German blunt force helped by the dominance of their gun lines, the aggression of their armoured assets and the ferocity of their infantry began to exert increasing pressure on the perimeter, forcing it to shrink. However, its reduction was controlled as there was plenty of fight still left in the defenders. Theirs was a stubborn resistance; fighting against heavy odds, they were either going to succeed extraordinarily or suffer a spectacular defeat. Their manner, type and style of fighting would not tolerate any mediocrity. Preventing German ground attacks that breached the perimeter from being pressed home on occasion involved sharp hand-to-hand, close-quarter fighting, the sort of fighting that brings a basic brutality with it. In such kill-or-be-killed situations, these one-to-one encounters demanded a deadly efficiency to kill, quick reactions and a strength and stamina of the variety that kept you alive, not your enemy.

German Royal Tiger tanks had arrived to Arnhem with the 503rd Heavy Panzer Battalion, increasing the armoured threat significantly. This danger had to be met head on and because the PIAT was a direct line of fire weapon it took a certain form of fatalism to put oneself forward in line of sight and make oneself vulnerable to the tank's fire or from its machine-guns and those of the support infantry. To suppress the reality of the risk, if making yourself susceptible to harm from a hailstorm of possibly pinpoint accurate fire in order to get your shot off meant believing that whatever was going to happen was inescapable and surrendering to that perhaps predestined occurrence was what it took, then so be it. Not everyone could do that, but there were those amongst them who would.

The newcomers, those who had not been in action before, were now well and truly blooded. Under attack from the time of their arrival and under constant fire since – at times intensely – and seeing three-quarters of their strength 'put out of battle' killed, wounded or captured, the Airborne Division were coping well and boys had become men. Having received a sharp baptism of fire within hours of their arrival, it was further forged on the crucible that Arnhem was turning out to be. They were proving silently heroic and resilient in the face of extreme and increasing hostility.

As long as the defenders had ammunition they were willing to use it, yet it was to supply ammunition to this readily disposed preparedness to continue to fight that was becoming an issue, as amounts were becoming scarce. Resupply was both the answer and the problem. The RAF were successfully risking harm dropping supplies, only the correctly designated drop zones had been overrun by the Germans and were now out of reach of the defenders, who had to watch helplessly as their supplies ended up in German hands. With radios not working there was no means to correct the situation, and although a small portion (10 per cent) dropped tantalisingly close to the defenders, most of that was still just out of reach. Supplies and ammunition needed to be collected and distributed and it was here that County Kilkenny man Michael Briody, Regimental Sergeant Major (R.S.M.) of the Glider Pilot Regiment stepped in and did what was necessary. In so doing, he earned the Dutch Bronze Star, the citation for which read:

> R.S.M. Briody throughout displayed splendid devotion to duty and untiring energy in maintaining the efficient working of supplies and ammunition, food and water, without which the unit could not have maintained its position. R.S.M. Briody exposed himself to every form of fire to collect supplies from containers and to deliver them to where they were most needed and his unfailing cheerfulness and energy was an inspiration to all who came in contact with him. Finally, when wounded by a mortar bomb splinter, he continued to display great unselfishness and insisted on remaining with his Wing, and finally succeeded in reaching safety when the withdrawal was ordered. This Warrant Officer's continual devotion to duty and bravery was exceptional.

In addition, in 1945 he was commissioned into the Royal Army Service Corps and received an MBE:

> R.S.M. Briody joined the Glider Pilot Regiment soon after its formation. Through his keenness, initiative, and devotion to duty on the Parade Ground, in the air and during Military Training, he has contributed very largely to the successful growth of the Regiment and to its outstanding achievements during operations. R.S.M. Briody served with the Regiment in Africa and Italy and was a splendid example to all. He piloted a Horsa to Arnhem in September 1944,

landed successfully and fought with gallantry for eight days. For over 3 years R.S.M. Briody has been an inspiration to all ranks and the present position of the Glider Pilot Regiment is in no small measure due to his tireless efforts.

In actuality, R.S.M. Briody had some difficulty getting to Arnhem and failed to reach it on the first day. He flew to Arnhem with the First Lift in Horsa Glider 185, with Staff Sergeant Marshall as his co-pilot and twenty-eight troops from No. 17 Platoon C Company, 1st Border Battalion. As the glider neared Braintree in Essex, poor visibility and a fracturing tow rope forced Briody to cast off. Only one of the ropes fell free while the other swung about as they made their descent and repeatedly struck the glider's fuselage. Briody and Marshall made a safe, albeit dramatic landing near RAF Andrews Field airfield, also known as RAF Great Sailing, which was used by B-26 Marauders of the 322nd Bomb Group. The landing was heavy and the glider passed through two fields and a hedge before it came to rest in a tangled wire fence. Nobody on board was hurt and while the men of No. 17 Platoon, depressed at the turn of events, unloaded the glider, Briody and Platoon Commander Lieutenant Bob Crittenden went to the airfield to seek assistance. They met an American Colonel who was extremely helpful. Crittenden had to refuse an invitation to dinner, as they had to return to base at the earliest opportunity, but the Colonel arranged to load the Platoon, together with their handcart, into several of his Marauders to fly them home. All but one man flew to Arnhem with the Second Lift on the following day.

There was also drama that day for the occupants of the glider trailing Dakota KG-328, with co-pilot RAF Warrant Officer Albert 'Bert' Smith, from County Armagh, and navigator Flying Officer Henry McKinley, born in Belfast but having grown up in America. Not long after arriving over Dutch airspace they encountered anti-aircraft fire and Warrant Officer Smith's Dakota was hit by flak. The pilot was killed instantly by a piece of shrapnel and Warrant Officer Smith momentarily knocked unconscious. Coming to his senses he found the Dakota climbing at an alarming rate and on the verge of stalling. Regaining control, he noticed that all of the crew had been wounded to some degree by the explosive burst of the anti-aircraft shell and neither had the aircraft itself escaped damage. He struggled to maintain level flight with a damaged port (left) engine but the aircraft began to lose height. Behind them, the glider they were towing was also damaged but with the return of the Dakota to level flight the glider pilot, Major John Blatch, reacted immediately and cast off. After an incredibly steep diving turn, Major Blatch landed the glider safely. Now Warrant Officer Bert Smith had now to do the same with the damaged Dakota. He turned the aircraft back towards England and, aided by his navigator Henry McKinley, prepared the Dakota for landing. He had never landed a Dakota solo before, but as RAF Martlesham Heath, an airfield in Suffolk used by the USAAF Eighth Air Force close to the British coast, came into view he made for that. It had a long runway and he used every inch of it – and more – as he brought the Dakota to a safe halt in the grass at the end of the runway, passing through a row of parked American fighter aircraft as he did so. For their actions both Warrant Officer Albert Smith, and Flying Officer Henry McKinley were awarded the Distinguished Flying Cross.

In September, 1944, Flying Officer McKinley and Warrant Officer Smith were navigator and map reader respectively in an aircraft detailed for a glider towing mission. The target was in Holland. When over enemy positions the aircraft was hit by anti-aircraft fire. The pilot was killed and Flying Officer McKinley was wounded. Despite this, he unhesitatingly went to assist his comrade, Warrant Officer Smith who, with great promptitude and resource had taken over the controls and was keeping the aircraft on its course towards the target.

The glider had been badly damaged and later its pilot was compelled to release. Warrant Officer Smith afterwards flew the aircraft back to an airfield where he effected a landing without incurring any further damage to the aircraft. Throughout the return flight, Flying

Officer McKinley, though suffering much pain, displayed the greatest determination and his accurate navigation was an important factor in the safe return of the aircraft. These members of aircraft crew set a fine example of courage and resource in the face of great difficulties.

Citation for the Distinguished Flying Cross awarded to Flying Officer Henry McKinley and Warrant Officer Albert Smith, 31 October 1944.

Five days later and four days behind schedule, with an improvement in the weather the Third Lift of paratroopers and glider-borne infantry finally took to the skies. The US 82nd and 101st Airborne Divisions were now rendered complete. Included also was the arrival by road via Normandy of their 'seaborne tail' complements. With these reinforcements and elements of the British Guards Armoured Division they were able to repulse further German attempts to cut the route on Hell's Highway and get the split convoy advancing once more. They were also able to move up vital supplies of ammunition, especially to the stalled armoured regiments and the much reduced 'fire missions' in the 64th Medium Regiment in support of the troops in the Oosterbeek perimeter.

Inside the perimeter the Airborne Division was trapped in the 'pocket', and the German attackers squeezed it smaller and smaller. Faced with this ruthlessness, the Airborne defenders fought back with a ferocity, energy and accuracy of their own, one that was to characterise their performance. One such example of this was the action of Staff Sergeant James Frederick 'Paddy' Boyd, the stowaway of B Squadron Glider Pilot Regiment. Not wanting to miss out on the action he had stowed away on board a flight during the First Lift on 17 September. Now, seven days later, he was amongst those positioned in their area of responsibility along the perimeter south of the Tafelberg Hotel. Part of a fighting patrol sent out that evening to harass the Germans and maintain an offensive spirit among the defenders they walked into a firefight. During the skirmish, the Germans had the best of the early exchanges and 'Paddy' Boyd was shot in the head. A colleague ran to his assistance, only to suffer fatal wounds too. The patrol, forced to withdraw, left the bodies behind them. After the battle, their field graves were discovered, but there is no known grave for Lance Corporal Thomas Dunbar from the Republic of Ireland, a member of the 21st Independent Parachute Company who was also killed in action on 23 September.

Private Richard Earls from County Carlow, a member of the 2nd Parachute Battalion, continued to fight on and survived the battle, making good his escape across the Rhine some days later. Another who survived but was taken prisoner of war was Private James 'Jimmy' Finn from Dundalk, County Louth. He had served in the Irish Defence Forces until the outbreak of war when he travelled to England to enlist. He subsequently joined the 10th Parachute Battalion and at some point returned to Ireland. There he was arrested as a deserter but treated with sympathy and given an immediate discharge. An Irish Defence Forces Officer told him, 'I don't blame you for going – if I had been twenty years younger I'd go myself.' Jimmy served at Arnhem and was badly beaten when captured. After the war he settled in Leicestershire with his wife, Doris. Jimmy died in 2001 and Doris in 2002.

There were also those in Arnhem who did not fight the Germans but did combat the wounds they inflicted. Amongst them was Private H. 'Paddy' Finnegan from the Republic of Ireland, a member of the Royal Army Medical Corps attached to the Headquarters Regimental Aid Post, and Private James 'Paddy' Flynn 1st Battalion Border Regiment, who served at Arnhem as a medical orderly in No. 18 Platoon C Company and was taken prisoner. Also born in Ireland was Captain Brian Devlin of the 181 Airlanding Field Ambulance Royal Army Medical Corps, the son of Doctor F.J. Devlin of Liverpool. In Operation Market Garden he was attached to the 7th Battalion, King's Own Scottish Borderers. He ended his career in the rank of Lieutenant Colonel and was awarded the OBE. These compassionate men of medicine and mercy, and others like them, held their ground to treat those who suffered wounds in a situation growing ever more perilous. Men who were starved, parched and exhausted, who were fighting with minimal ammunition, no reinforcements, very limited resupply and no air cover.

On the seventh day there was a perceptible change in the German attack methodology. During the course of each day, they began to stand off more noticeably and using artillery, tanks and self-propelled anti-tank guns in combination with flamethrowers systematically began destroying Airborne 'strong points' and employed less use of infantry. Late evening, from his headquarters in the Hartenstein Hotel in the centre of the perimeter, Major General Roy Urquhart, 1st Airborne Division Commander, radioed Lieutenant General 'Boy' Browning at this Tactical Headquarters to the effect:

> Numerous attacks by infantry, supported by self-propelled guns, tanks and even flamethrowers. All attacks accompanied by heavy shelling and mortaring. Headquarters are also battered. Situation inside the perimeter largely unchanged but positions now more thinly manned. Still no contact with our forces on the south bank. Air supply a failure. Have recovered only a small amount of ammunition. No rations so far. Because of scarcity of water all ranks rather filthy. Morale still high but heavy bombardment is showing signs of effect. Will hold out but looking forward to better days.

It seemed the smaller the perimeter became, the more obstinate were the men of the British Airborne. They continued to defend every ruin and fought over every inch of ground.

10

AGAINST ALL ODDS (24 SEPTEMBER 1944)

Bombarded from all sides at once, the impacts of the ferocious barrage sent dirt and debris flying through the air. Thick swirls of dust and smoke blocked the vision of the Airborne troops as explosions scattered masonry, soil and shrapnel haphazardly in all directions. The noise was thunderous and incessant, a persistent percussion calculated to be oppressive and disorienting. The continuing series of detonations sucked the air from around them, the bomb bursts stifling and the explosions suffocating. Dramatic, debilitating and desperate, the eighth day of Operation Market Garden saw the German forces launch a blatant, blistering bludgeoning of the perimeter.

Artillery, tanks and mortars hammered the Airborne pocket from early morning and all throughout the day. Impatient for success, the Germans were becoming eager for victory and increasingly intolerant of resistance. They wanted to obliterate the opposition and were uncompromising in their attempt to overwhelm the defenders; to inflict on Urquhart and his men at Oosterbeek what they had imposed on Lieutenant Colonel 'Johnny' Frost and his men at the bridge – only to far greater effect. They were giving vent to their desire to overcome the Airborne with incessant artillery shells, mortar bombs and tank rounds. They were determined to deliver a helter-skelter haranguing overload of the senses that would leave them dead or otherwise distraught.

Under this incessant pressure, but well dug in – sheltering in slit trenches or protected by partially-fortified strong points in now ruined houses and shattered streets – the defenders were ready for another day's hate and hostility, to once more roll the dice of fate, defy the odds and stand strong. Shoulder-deep in adversity, they were prepared to handle the hardships, address the adversity and continue to fight. In action for a week already and without rest, reinforcements or resupply, the Airborne were not yet prepared to admit they were destined for defeat. Although their position was decidedly vulnerable, the barrage remorseless and the situation perilous, amazingly their reserves of resilience were not yet exhausted or their reservoirs of endurance expended.

There was no false bravado, one could not be anything but afraid, yet their survival instinct was too strong. This extreme exposure to danger gave rise to fear and made each soldier aware of the basic elements of the self, of the tension between finding oneself in a terrifying ongoing situation and not wanting to be there, of the strain of being in jeopardy and instead wanting to be safe. Theirs was a struggle for courage, lost, then found again all in one moment, and there were many such moments. Every man felt it, not many showed it, but all shared it. Character, competence and camaraderie sustained them and it was this control of fear that conspicuously championed their defence of the perimeter.

Good leadership also combats fear, an essential part of which is being visible. Being seen, not sitting hidden in a corner but being out and about, is reassuring and the troops knew that their commanders saw and shared what was happening around them. All the better also to estimate what was coming, and this built trust between the troops and the leadership and from this credibility came confidence. Moving from position to position, Brigadier General John 'Shan' Hackett encouraged, rallied and gave heart to the Airborne troops. He was calm and deliberate and his controlled unexcitable nature was infectious. He knew the Germans thought they would give up, and that the Airborne troops had not was perplexing them. Good men had died and good work had been done by holding out; it was not a situation that was going to be easily given up. He also knew that the situation was not going to resolve itself, so for his part he would do whatever he could to protect and rally his troops, as he had demonstrated the Wednesday beforehand as the instigator of the action at what became known as Hackett's Hollow. Before the reckless yet incredible charge that day, Hackett had been seen running through the woods as a hail of enemy fire erupted around him to where three jeeps were located. One of the vehicles was on fire, next to another stacked with ammunition that could explode at any moment. On the third was a badly wounded casualty strapped to a stretcher. Braving the German gunfire and the flames of the burning jeep, and the potential of being blown up by the ammunition in the second, he jumped into the third vehicle and drove it and the casualty to safety. The wounded man, whose life he undoubtedly saved, turned out to be Lieutenant Colonel Derick Heathcoat-Amory, later Harold Macmillan's Chancellor of the Exchequer.

After the incessant 'thud, bang! thud, bang! thud bang!' of mortars impacting and exploding, there was suddenly silence. An acute silence, a momentary dizzy but deep silence, and the only disturbance was their own thoughts; surely no one could have survived that, but they had. The Airborne began to wonder, was it actually over? They strained their ears and tentatively peered out of the trenches. Was it just a lull, will the barrage start up again or a misfire belatedly explode? It appeared to be over and Brigadier 'Shan' Hackett moved on, continuing his daily tour of inspection of perimeter positions. Then, as he scrambled amongst the debris along the perimeter the mortaring restarted, the explosions seemingly following him as he moved. Only this time he did not get into cover fast enough and a mortar bomb impact falling close by caught him. He was lacerated in the leg and stomach with shrapnel slivers, causing serious internal injuries. 'Shan' Hackett's fight was over, and in the circumstances with a stomach wound his life might well have been too. He lost consciousness, only awakening to find himself in St Elisabeth Hospital being prodded by the toecap of a German surgeon who was unimpressed with the likelihood of his chances of survival and was not inclined to treat him. Fortunately, Alexander Lipmann-Kessel ('Lippy'), a British Army doctor of South African descent, operated on Brigadier Hackett and successfully removed some twenty pieces of shrapnel from his stomach. Meanwhile, back along the length of perimeter it was now the responsibility of Lieutenant Colonel Ian Murray of the Glider Pilot Regiment, to assume command and control.

Lieutenant General Brian Horrocks, conscious that it was now the eighth day of an operation that was to have lasted two to three days at most, was not for giving up either. He knew that many soldiers were involved in getting this far and they were tantalisingly close to successfully completing the Operation. He ordered XXX Corps artillery to lend fire support to the beleaguered defenders and close air support missions were flown by the 2nd Tactical Air Force from mid-afternoon, despite problems identifying targets in the ever-shrinking Oosterbeek perimeter. The Poles had made their third, but ultimately unsuccessful, nightly attempt to ferry reinforcements across the Rhine during the early hours of darkness only for their positions on the south bank to be targeted by German artillery. Once more the RAF tried to resupply the 1st Airborne Division, but again to no good effect. Yet neither collapsing from exhaustion, nor hesitating due to lack of ammunition, the Airborne fought on and the perimeter continued to be held.

Men like Private Samuel John Kendrick from Bridgetown, County Wexford, 1st Parachute Battalion; M. Leese from Courtmacsherry, County Cork, 156 Parachute Battalion; Lance Sergeant John 'Jack' Fryer from Northern Ireland, 1st Parachute Battalion; Private Frank McCormick from Dublin, 1st Parachute Battalion (who may have served with his friend Tom Gerraghty from Carrick-on-Suir, County Tipperary, under the name of McCluskey), and Private Thomas Wilson from Belfast, 2nd Battalion, South Staffordshire Regiment. Although hassled, harried and hungry, these Irish troopers – amongst the many others – displayed grit and determination and, if not completely unfazed, were nonetheless unfaltering in defence. Late in the day a medical truce was arranged and 700 wounded were transferred to the Germans (some 500 more the following day), leaving less than 2,000 men to defend the perimeter.

Lieutenant General Brian Horrocks, Commander XXX Corps, Major General Ivor Thomas commanding 43rd (Wessex) Division, leading elements of which had arrived at Driel to support the Poles, and Major General Stanisław Sosabowski, Commander 1st Polish Parachute Brigade, climbed the steep steps of the steeple of Driel church and studied the terrain around them, conducting an operational appreciation of the situation. It seemed that unless something could be done to force the present circumstances to change, the annihilation of the 1st Airborne Division – or what remained of it – was imminent. With defeat staring the Allies in the face, it was decided that the main objective of Operation Market Garden, to cross the Rhine and set up a 'start line' for an advance into Germany, was to be abandoned and a new defensive line would be established at Nijmegen. It seemed a planned withdrawal from the perimeter may be necessary.

Hell's Highway was certainly not immune from attack, and the US 82nd and 101st Airborne in particular had to repulse a series of German assaults throughout the day. At dusk, German troops from Kampfgruppe Chill under the command of Generalleutnant Kurt Chill eventually succeeded in cutting the route just south of Veghel, near Koevering. This was not the only German movement; further fresh reinforcements arrived in the form of the 506th Heavy Tank Battalion with some sixty King Tiger tanks. Half went to the blocking position at Elst on the Arnhem–Nijmegen road, the other half headed for the east side of the Oosterbeek perimeter. For the defenders, by the end of the eighth day an already grim situation was turning dire.

Along Hell's Highway, the corridor was under threat and successfully cut by the Germans for a while, the significance of such interference being the splitting and halting of convoys and hence a delay to the arrival of essential supplies to support the fierce fighting to remove the blockage on the route further north, which was south of Arnhem at Elms. The attention of the Guards Armoured Division, or elements thereof, was directed to restore control of the corridor, with British ground troops at times giving infantry support to these tanks. Rifleman John Shanahan from Cork, a member of 2nd Battalion of the Royal Ulster Rifles who had come ashore on Sword Beach on D-Day at Normandy and fought alongside his comrades in many battles since, was once again in action, fighting in support of the big advance on Arnhem. In the course of the supporting action, Rifleman Shanahan was caught in a mine blast triggered by a heavy tank. John was blinded by the blast and taken back to England through Nijmegen and Brussels. Thankfully, after hospital treatment in South Shields, John's sight was restored.

Another Irishman in action during Operation Market Garden was Airborne Trooper James Flanagan, but he wore a US 101st uniform as a member of the 502nd Parachute Infantry Company. He too was a D-Day veteran, who landed pre-H-Hour behind and inland of Utah Beach near Ravenoville with the aim of clearing and keeping removed any German resistance along the vulnerable causeways that led inland from the beach. Along with other US paratroopers, he had successfully assaulted a German command post at Marmion's Farm and afterwards was photographed by an International News Service photographer with the captured German swastika flag. The photograph, with James Flanagan in the centre of the group of 101st Airborne holding the flag, was wired back to the United States and became one of the most widely distributed newspaper photographs taken from the events of D-Day. He was later involved in the taking of Carentan before performing clearance of booby traps and mines – location, defusing and removal – in Cherbourg. At the end of June he was picked up by a landing craft and taken back to England.

Now in action again, this time fighting around Sint-Oedenrode, James Flanagan was wounded in the 'seven jeeps episode'. A Colonel from another US outfit, not an Airborne officer, was proceeding up an unsecured road with seven jeeps, which had been flown in earlier by glider. Having been warned by an MP at an intersection that the road he was about to take was not secure or safe to travel he proceeded anyway, and soon met German resistance. The lead jeep was hit and destroyed and the group was forced to abandon their caravan under enemy fire. They made it safely back to Sint-Oedenrode on foot, whereupon the Colonel asked James Flanagan's Platoon Commander that he recover the seven jeeps. Acting as a scout, James Flanagan was out in front (known as 'on point') of this recovery detail, moving along a ditch alongside the road where the jeeps were located. As he neared a typical Dutch house along the road, he noticed a window was open and the curtains pulled back. An experienced soldier by this time, having seen action in Normandy, it looked suspicious and he aimed his M1 Garand rifle, the weapon of the US infantryman, at the window. His hunch was right and the scout group soon discovered there was a German MG 42 machine-gun in the building. He fired eight rounds into the window and the firing from the MG 42 ceased. However, the German machine gunners were supported by a mortar battery and this became apparent when 50 yards ahead of him mortar rounds began crashing around his ditch. With precision, the mortar fire impacts were 'walking back' towards him, starting fire at one end of a target area and then systematically moving the fire across the target. He pressed himself tightly into the ditch, desperately seeking cover, but the mortar impacts proceeded steadily in his direction until one exploded next to him. The force was so great it propelled him out of the ditch and blew the stock clean off his M1 rifle. He was hit by shrapnel in about three dozen places, in his arms, legs and ribs. A medic attended to him and gave him a shot of morphine, and with the physical aid of the medic he partially walked back to safety and hospitalisation in Sint-Oedenrode. He was there for four or five days before transportation via Brussels to England a number of days later.

This wasn't the end of the war for Trooper James Flanagan. After two months recovering in an Army hospital in England he was returned to his unit in France several days before the Battle of the Bulge (16 December 1944–25 January 1945), the last major German offensive campaign on the Western Front during the Second World War. During this action he came down with frostbite and after spending a further two weeks in hospital was returned to duty and spent the remainder of the war mopping up German resistance. After the conclusion of hostilities he was returned to the US in December 1945 then moved to California and pursued his interest in the aviation industry. James Wallace Flanagan died in Auburn, Placer County, California on 8 December 2005, aged 82.

Very much in action during Operation Market Garden were the Irish Guards Armoured Division. Having come ashore in Normandy not long after D-Day, they had been involved in some serious warfare as they battled their way through France, Belgium and now all the way up and along the corridor. One of those was Captain Charles Barton Tottenham from Ballycurry, Ashford, County Wicklow (born in Mount Callan, County Clare), who had fought in the relief of Belgium and was awarded an MC (gazetted 1 March 1945) for an action near the village of Hechtel in Belgium. During heavy fighting from 6–12 September 1944, just prior to Operation Market Garden, his tank was knocked out and he took over another, and the events that unfolded are described in his citation:

On Sunday morning, 10 September 1944, No. 2 Squadron were ordered to attack, in support of No. 4 Company, 3rd Battalion Irish Guards, west of the strongly held village of Hechtel. The country was very thick with visibility thirty yards, and there was no opportunity for reconnaissance. Lieutenant Tottenham commanded the leading troop in this attack and led off through the pinewoods on a compass bearing. Contact between troops was quite impossible. Lieutenant Tottenham soon lost one tank, bogged, but continued on with his other tank, and took up position dominating the main road. He at once came under fire from two anti-tank guns and a self-propelled gun. One anti-tank gun was knocked out by another tank when Lieutenant Tottenham's tank was hit on the gun. Lieutenant Tottenham quickly changed tanks. In this, his remaining tank, he then engaged three enemy Mark IVs and knocked out one.

Entirely alone and unsupported, sniped by enemy infantry, he continued to hold this dominating position, knocking out another anti-tank gun. It was thirty minutes before he was joined by the rest of his Squadron.

Lieutenant Tottenham's skill in maintaining direction, accurate marksmanship, and will and determination to engage the enemy were of the highest order and were of the greatest value to the success of this operation.

Also busy soldiering with the 'Micks' was Lieutenant John Gorman from Omagh, County Tyrone, who was commissioned into the 2nd Battalion Irish Guards, later becoming part of the 5th Guards Armoured Brigade, Guards Armoured Division, who had previously won a Military Cross (MC) for disabling a German tank by ramming it with his own Sherman tank. The *War Diary of the Irish Guards*, whose function was to give a brief account of events, tells us that:

Orders were received from the Brigade Commander for the Battalion to pass through the 2 Armoured Grenadier Guards, take over Cagny and push on to Vimont. The order of march was No. 2 Squadron, No.1 Squadron, Battalion HQ, No. 3 Squadron. En route Lieutenant A.E. Dorman destroyed a SP 7.5 in full retreat. No. 1 Squadron then crossed the stream running north from Cagny and moved up the [far side of the] ridge ... with the objective of [taking the] crossroads by Frénouville. Lieutenant J. Gorman's troop on the left literally ran into 3 panzers just over the crest. Lieutenant Gorman rammed one – he was too close and the Panzers too surprised for either to shoot – jumped out and led his crew back to Cagny. Lance Sergeant Harbinson in the following tank was hit as he crossed the Cagny–Émiéville road and was badly wounded himself. Of his crew, Lance Corporal Watson and Guardsman Davis were killed and Guardsman Walsh and Guardsman Melville wounded. Of Lieutenant Gorman's crew, Guardsman Agnew and Guardsman Scholes were slightly wounded. Back by the orchard, Lieutenant Gorman found Lance Sergeant Workman's

93

'Firefly' (a Sherman tank with powerful 17-pound anti-tank gun). Lance Sergeant Workman had just been killed, though the tank was intact, so Lieutenant Gorman pulled out the body and returned … to the battle. Lieutenant A.E. Dorman had by now reached the ridge and between them they shot up the 2 remaining Panzers.

It appears that the German Panzers' in question may well have been one of the formidable Tiger II heavy tanks. Promoted to Captain, John Gorman took part in Operation Market Garden with the Irish Guards, a leading part of the ground phase of the Operation. Gorman's tanks reached the bridge at Nijmegen before the Operation was called off. Here, at the operation's end, he shared the despair of being unable to proceed with tanks past Elst along the elevated 'island' highway running due north to Arnhem, a difficult – or as it proved, impossible – place to operate armoured vehicles. Although it had been possible to manoeuvre off the main road, on the 'island' this was not possible as the route ran along a dyke embankment and the ground around it was too soft to take the weight of the tanks. This elevated narrow roadway also silhouetted the tanks, presenting an unmissable target for German self-propelled anti-tank guns. Coming under fire the advance came to a halt. Captain Gorman knew that with no air support, no artillery support and no infantry support, they would have to sit there and wait. John Gorman shared the wretchedness of their helplessness, articulating it as follows: 'We had come all the way from Normandy, taken Brussels, fought halfway through Holland and crossed the Nijmegen bridge. Arnhem and those paratroopers were just up ahead and, almost in sight of that last bloody bridge, we were stopped. I never felt such morbid despair.' Meanwhile, at Oosterbeek what was left of the 1st Airborne Division were fighting for their lives.

11

OPERATION BERLIN (25-26 SEPTEMBER 1944)

Shell-shattered houses in bomb-cratered gardens, ruined rubble-strewn streets, and all around them debris. The intensity and duration of the fighting had led to a dreadful amount of death and destruction for the 1st Airborne Division. Bombarded by artillery and mortars, targeted by tanks, and now penetrated by infantry, the perimeter at Oosterbeek was compressed to a pocket, roughly one mile by half a mile (1,500 by 900 metres) in size. The failure of XXX Corps to push to Arnhem from Nijmegen on the fourth day (20 September), when up to nightfall the highly exposed single dyke road was still largely undefended – only for it to be reinforced and blocked by German defences – was likely the decisive moment of the success or failure of the Operation. Had the Guards Armoured Division tried a little harder, then perhaps the outcome – so tantalisingly close to a successful conclusion – might not have been thwarted.

That too little account had been taken of the seriousness of the position of the Airborne Division in the Cauldron was the Allies undoing. The slow moving and largely unsupported British VIII and XII Corps, as they advanced up the flanks of the salient – the large area of land protruding through the German lines controlled by the Allies – within which was the desperately defended corridor, also contributed to the failure to seize their ultimate objective. Bad weather, bad planning, and other reasons had led the Allies to where they were now. The requirements of the US IX Carrier Command's Air Plan shaped how the airlift was to proceed, and considerations regarding aircraft survivability seemed to outweigh those of airborne insertion – either en masse or the proposed two-lift option on Day One – as did the selection of distant drop and landing zone locations from their objectives. In addition, Major General Paul Williams' decision not to allow close air fighter and fighter-bomber support during insertion and resupply only contributed to weakening the entire operation. Ironically, the furthest airlift – that of Urquhart's British 1st Airborne Division to Arnhem – was also the smallest. And so, with the smallest force he had both to attack the prize objective whilst also defending the landing and drop zones. Finally, and perhaps vitally, the failure of the Operation's planners to respond to disturbing intelligence reports coming from both the Dutch underground and Allied interceptions of German communications, and concerns from officers such as Polish Airborne Brigade Commander Stanisław Sosabowski, about the German strength, composition and intent, led to the Allied forces being placed in an unwinnable position.

The known German situation was oversimplified and too many people had 'skin in the game' to see it tackled effectively: the US Allied Commanders wished to see what the First Allied Airborne Army (FAAA) could accomplish; Churchill wanted to see destroyed the Vergeltungswaffen ('V' for Vengeance) V-1 and V-2 launching sites in the Netherlands; Montgomery wanted to regain control of Allied strategy; Brereton and Browning wanted desperately to be seen to have operational airborne experience, and General Eisenhower wanted an end to the squabbling between his rival subordinates and secure a Rhine crossing. The Airborne Division commanders themselves, most especially Major General Roy Urquhart, British 1st Airborne Division, were less discerning than they should have been but the truth of the matter was they were anxious to get into action. They wanted to earn their airborne spurs, to do what they were trained for and prevent the troops becoming bored, but they really ought to have been more questioning of their superiors as to the actual risks involved. In truth, they were battle-hungry. These and other contributory factors had led them to their present position.

There had still been opportunities to turn matters around, perhaps when the 1st Independent Polish Parachute Brigade dropped successfully into Driel, only there was no ferry or any other useful means available to cross the river. Continued delays in getting enough assault boats where needed, due to the route being cut by the Germans, also fatally frustrated the effort and the loss of the high ground at Westerbouwing on the north side of the Lower Rhine above Heveadorp was also significant. The defensive stand of the Airborne Division had been magnificent: the more compact the perimeter, the more defiant they became, so that right to the end they kept the option open, however slight, of a successful bridgehead across the Lower Rhine. Simultaneously, with the scent of victory in the air the Germans hastily reinforced, enlarged and resupplied an already substantial garrison.

Trying hard too were the Poles, and fighting with distinction alongside them was Irishman Private W. 'Paddy' Cooney of the 2nd Parachute Battalion and Sergeant Eric Matson from Bandon, County Cork, of the Glider Pilot Regiment, who supported the Polish Brigade in fighting off German attacks from Elst on their eastern flank. Allied frustration to support the 1st Airborne Division turned to desperation, in turn unfortunately leading to miscalculation. General Urquhart had sent Lieutenant Colonel Charles Mackenzie and Lieutenant Colonel Eddie Myers, his Chief of Staff and Chief Engineer Officer respectively, over the river to talk with General 'Boy' Browning. By then no fewer than three valiant attempts had been made by the Poles to cross the Lower Rhine to Heveadorp and reinforce the perimeter, but each had been largely unsuccessful. Now a more elaborate plan, including sending soldiers of the Dorsetshire Regiment alongside the Poles, was hatched to prevent the complete collapse of the Airborne Division's position. The orders for the Battalion read:

> C.O. 'O' GP intentions are that the Battalion will cross river Nederrijn at Ferry and enlarge the Bridge Head already held by Parachutists also to get supplies through to the Airborne Troops. A+B Companies to be in first flight of assault boats followed by C+D Companies. Then TAC Batallion [*sic*] H.Q. followed by S Company Personnel with

supplies. Batallion to have support of 3 Regiments of party together with 4.2 Mortars and M.Gs (machine-guns).

General Sosabowski was not optimistic about the plan and suggested it be moved further west, where German resistance was less intense. However, he was ignored and in the event only sufficient amphibious craft for two companies – 350 men – of the 4th Battalion of the Dorsetshire Regiment made the river crossing. Although the crossings went undetected at first, the light provided by two buildings set light by XXX Corps artillery barrage revealed the boats making the crossing and the Germans, who had realised the Allies were making crossings and set themselves up in defensive positions overlooking likely crossing points, opened fire. One boat was sunk but just over 300 troops reached the far bank, who immediately found themselves pinned down by German machine-guns and grenade attacks. Approximately 150 prisoners, including the battalion commander, were taken, including County Meath man D.L. Eccles, a soldier in the Dorsetshire Regiment.

At this stage, the choice for the 1st Airborne Division was annihilation or evacuation. Effectively, Operation Market Garden was finished when the Allied commanders decided to abandon the planned crossing of the Rhine and set up defensive positions in Nijmegen the day before and an evacuation plan, codenamed Operation Berlin, had now to be prepared. The ironically named plan was set to commence at 2200 hours (10 pm) under the cover of darkness with a decoy river crossing to confuse the Germans. However, there was still a full day's fighting to be engaged with before then. It was a day that saw the newly arrived Tiger II tanks brought into play and the perimeter's width further compressed to 600 metres from one side to the other, when determined defence met and held further fierce assault. It also saw Lance Corporal Ernest Lynas from County Armagh, of the 156 Parachute Battalion, killed in action. But hold they did, with the aid of artillery and close air support sorties.

The close-quarter exchanges that day at Oosterbeek and in Arnhem throughout the overall battle were a series of ferocious small-scale actions. It was frightening and exciting, dreadful and stirring all at once. They were brutal, grim and grave skirmishes for sure, but they were also dramatic. And there is no bigger drama than that of the fine balance between life and death, the ultimate, extreme and fundamental moment that sees the end of an individual's existence. In such circumstances there was a role for the chaplains, who tended to the casualties and to those dying of their wounds. Comforting Lieutenant Colonel John Dutton 'Johnny' Frost's men at the bridge was Father Bernard Egan as, exhausted and filthy with bloodshot and red-rimmed eyes, they put up their stubborn and fearless resistance, until he himself became a victim of the overwhelming, tank, self-propelled and artillery shellfire. When a shell struck the building he was in, Father Egan fell two storeys from a stairwell into a room which was once again struck, this time knocking him unconscious. When he came around, the room was on fire and he found it difficult to move. Fortunately, he was rescued by Lieutenant 'Bucky' Buchanan, who passed him out the window into the arms of a sergeant below. Lieutenant Buchanan's namesake, no relation, was the Reverend Captain Alan Alexander Buchanan from Fintona, County Tyrone, who served as Padre to the 2nd Battalion South Staffordshire Regiment. Educated at Trinity College Dublin, he received a Mention in Dispatches for his work at Arnhem. Reverend Captain Buchanan was captured and became a POW in Stalag XI-B Fallingbostel. After the war he became Archbishop of Dublin. A memorial window was unveiled to him at Clogher Cathedral, County Tyrone, on 4 June 2000.

The Dutch population had been compassionate and supportive throughout Operation Market Garden, taking wounded British soldiers into their homes, tending to them, getting them to hospital and granting shelter in their cellars throughout the bombardments. Post-evacuation, at continued risk to themselves, they successfully concealed British survivors and, with the assistance of the Dutch underground resistance (the PAN), managed to get many safely back across the Lower Rhine. The Dutch underground had supplied much useful information to the Allies but, fearful that the underground was being infiltrated by German intelligence, not much was used. Offers to physically fight in support of the British were also declined, much to the underground's disappointment. However, post-Operation Market Garden, they rationalised that they still had an important role to play and remained active.

Finally, night came and it was time to leave. Word was filtered down to the sub-units within the perimeter. General Urquhart had decided he would shrink the perimeter from within, and those wounded who were too incapacitated to move (differing estimates of 400–500 men) assisted by a small rear guard including the Poles, would be given what ammunition was left and remain in contact with the enemy, as if resistance was continuing. To further add to this deception, at 2100 hours (9 pm) an almighty and sustained bombardment began by XXX Corps and 43rd Division guns, under the cover of which in the pitch darkness and pouring rain, the 1st Airborne Division started to withdraw. Royal Canadian Engineers with some twenty storm boats (each with a capacity for fourteen men) and two Royal Engineer companies with sixteen assault boats began to ferry the worn-out defenders, who made their way single file towards the river bank in long human chains, each man holding on to the smock-tail (a flap attached to the back hem of the paratrooper's smock intended to keep it in place during the jump. While more properly known as a 'crutch flap', the troops invariably named it after some form of tail) of the soldier in front, guided by white tape and members of the Glider Pilot Regiment.

Not all made it safely; some 170 were taken prisoner while others were killed or wounded by mortar fire. Close to one such unfortunate was Lance Corporal Tom 'Paddy' Breen from the Republic, 1st Airborne Provosts Company Corps of Military Police, who was wounded by the same shell. Hit in the face and head, he lay wounded by the roadside until discovered by the Germans the next morning and taken prisoner. Sergeant Peter Quinn from Athlone, County Westmeath, 1st Airborne Reconnaissance Squadron, also suffered the ill effects of an irregular mortar bomb blast. Blown off his feet, he recovered consciousness to find himself lying against the trunk of a tree. He scrambled towards the river bank, avoiding machine-gun fire and German sentries en route, when a second blast of mortar fire sent him sprawling again. This time he remained conscious long enough to notice the second-in-command of the Squadron being felled by a burst of machine-gun fire. Hoisting the wounded officer onto his shoulders, the river bank now only 200 metres away, he made a desperate dash and successfully managed to reach a waiting boat.

Those escaping across the Lower Rhine were not necessarily safe when they reached the river bank, because from there they had to cross the fast flowing 400-metre width of the Lower Rhine, sometimes under sweeping German machine-gun and mortar fire. Boats were sunk, people drowned and at 0600 hours (6 am) on Tuesday 26 September, when no more boats arrived to take those waiting across, they were faced with a choice: to stay and be captured or risk swimming and drown. Some stayed, some swam and made it across and some drowned. In all, Operation Berlin was a success and the Germans were largely unaware that the 1st Airborne Division were gone. Today, on the south bank of the Rhine is a monument commemorating the role of Canadian and British engineers who participated in Operation Berlin. The text on the monument reads as follows:

It is 25th September 1944: The battle of Arnhem is still raging, but the position of the surrounded British and Polish troops on the northern Rhine bank has become untenable. Then the order for their evacuation across the river is given. In that rainy night hundreds of soldiers come in small parties to the river forelands, between the farmhouse and the Old Church … and wait to be rescued. Under heavy German fire from the Westerbouwing, British (260 and 553 Field Companies) and Canadian (20 and 23 Field Companies) Engineers make dozens of trips in their small boats from this bank. In one night, supported by other units, they manage to rescue 2,400 airborne troops. At the time the rescued had hardly seen their savers, so they have never been able to thank them. This monument has been erected to express their gratitude

With the success of the evacuation Operation Market Garden came effectively to a close, only closed too was the back door to the Ruhr. Monty's plan had misfired, with the primary miscalculation involved in its execution perhaps being one of over optimism. Approximately 10,600 men of the 1st Airborne Division and other units had been parachuted into Holland. Of these approximately 2,400 were evacuated in Operation Berlin, 1,485 killed and 6,414 taken prisoner, of whom one third were wounded.

12

TELLING THE STORY OF OPERATION MARKET GARDEN

Montgomery's bold move to shorten the war by an audacious attack to capture and hold the vital bridges across the Lower Rhine, including that at Arnhem, was defeated. It had been a gigantic gamble and a desperately risky undertaking at best and it had ended in failure. Nonetheless, it was a gallant action and for nine days the Airborne Division held out against overwhelming odds in one of the most fiercely fought battles of the Second World War. Underestimating known German strength and their rapidity to concentrate reinforcements, it became a battle of bloody desperation, the defenders steadily dwindling as they fought off assault after determined assault, until defeat was inevitable. Those are the bare facts, but the details of this stirring story contain the very heartbeat of solid soldiering by self-reliant, forceful, direct, courageous and resourceful soldiers in an epic action. The campaign to free Europe from Nazi oppression received a setback at Arnhem which did prolong the war. Yet from within this harsh reality of defeat emerged a tale of success, of bravery and endurance over adversity: in short, a victory. And a large part of this acknowledgement is down to its telling.

One Irishman who was there and whose job it was to tell that story as it happened was Galway man Jack Smyth, a war correspondent for Reuters News Agency. A footnote in another Irishman's book about Arnhem, Dubliner Cornelius Ryan's *A Bridge Too Far* (1974), tells us:

Some of the war's finest reporting came out of Arnhem. The ten man Press team attached to the First Airborne Division included Major Roy Oliver, a Public Relations Officer, Censors Flight Lieutenant Billy Williams and Captain Peter Brett, army photographers Sergeant Lewis and Walker and correspondents Alan Wood, *Daily Express*, Stanley Maxted and Guy Byman, BBC, Jack Smyth, Reuters and Marek Święcicki, a Polish correspondent attached to Sosabowski's Brigade. Although limited to sparse communications, i.e. bulletins of only a few hundred words per day, these men, in the finest tradition of war reporting, portrayed the agonies of Urquhart's men. I have been unable to locate a single correspondent of the original team. Presumably all are dead.

Jack Smyth and his wife, Eileen, were tragically killed when their car accidentally plunged into the River Liffey on a cold December night in 1956. Born in Galway, Jack began his journalistic career at the *Connaught Tribune* before leaving for London in the early 1940s to join Reuters News Agency, where he undertook the dangerous role of a war correspondent. Without any parachute training he dropped into Arnhem with the 1st Airborne Division and at first hand witnessed and reported on events from the thick of the battle, one report including the following lines: 'On this fifth day, our force is still being heavily mortared, sniped, machine-gunned and shelled ... when the Second Army arrived and relieves this crowd, then may be told one of the epics of the war. In the meantime, they go on fighting their hearts out.'

On the very same day he finished that report, he was captured by the Germans and, believing him privy – as a war correspondent – to information possibly indicating further airborne operations, he was 'roughly interrogated' by the Gestapo. He was held for seventeen days then transferred to a prison camp, where he spent eight months, before being liberated by American troops. On his return he reportedly told a friend and fellow journalist: 'Jaysus, they beat the shit out of me! There was I, in British Army officer's uniform, telling 'em I was a neutral and demanding to see the nearest Irish ambassador. Well, they were having none of that.'

After Germany, he turned his attention to the East and was one of the first journalists to visit the ruined Hiroshima. He later worked for several newspapers in Ireland, including *The Waterford Star, Evening Press* and the *Irish Press*. Before the tragic accident that claimed his life and that of his wife, Jack wrote and published a book, *Five Days in Hell*, about his experiences at Arnhem.

A much more widely known book is the previously mentioned *A Bridge Too Far* by Cornelius Ryan from Dublin (also author of *The Longest Day* and *The Last Battle*). Like *The Longest Day*, Ryan's book about D-Day, *A Bridge Too Far* formed the basis for a major Hollywood production in 1976 of the same name. Directed by Richard Attenborough, with a budget of some $24 million and hosting an abundance of Hollywood's then biggest stars it was a good film for its time, though it tended to veer a little more towards entertainment than strict historical rigour. This raises the interesting question regarding setting an onus of responsibility on the film maker to relate realism and remain reliable, particularly with regard to getting the historical facts right and portraying them correctly.

In general, Attenborough's film of *A Bridge Too Far* is very faithful to history with regard to the identity of those involved and the events surrounding Operation Market Garden. The denial of intelligence reports by Lieutenant General 'Boy' Browning, commander of the airborne operation is portrayed, and Browning was shown as placing any officers who called for the Operation to be cancelled on sick leave, which was correct. The anger of the Dutch Resistance when their intelligence was ignored, was also shown. The movie was committed to show the real campaign and in general it does illustrate how the battle unfolded, though of course the full nine days of the campaign is somewhat simplified. The major characters in the film are based on real historical figures, including the German officers, though the one major character omitted from the movie is that of Field Marshal Bernard Montgomery, himself. Montgomery was the architect of Operation Market Garden and it is undeniable that without him it is unlikely the operation would have proceeded. Yet despite many references to Montgomery throughout the film it does not include him.

A Bloody Week

The 'look' of *A Bridge Too Far* is very 'Hollywood', and despite its gritty scenes and extravagant battle sequences there is no denying this is a 1970s blockbuster. In contrast, the opening sequence of Steven Spielberg's 1998 film *Saving Private Ryan* depicting the torrid scenes on Omaha Beach, which was filmed in Ireland at Ballinesker Beach and Curracloe Stand in County Wexford with over 2,500 Irish reserve army troops recruited to portray the Allied forces storming the beach, was modelled on actual newsreel footage from the era. The modern lenses of the film's cameras were converted to make them capture images more like those from the 1940s, and Spielberg and his cinematographer, Janusz Kamiński, also built the look of the D-Day sequence on the bleached-out grainy appearance of the D-Day photographs shot by Robert Capa. Indeed, so realistic was the film's opening sequence that the US Department of Veterans' Affairs set up a nationwide toll-free hotline for veterans and their family members to call if they felt unsettled by the events depicted on screen. Thereafter, the story becomes somewhat fictionalised, but such is the nature of the production of these spectacular box office-orientated extravaganzas.

Less well known nowadays is the 1946 film *Theirs is the Glory: Men of Arnhem* by the Rank Organisation, directed by Irishman Brian Desmond Hurst. A written statement at the start of the film reads: '*Theirs is the Glory* has been produced entirely without the use of studio sets or actors. Every incident was either experienced or witnessed by the people who appear in the film.' Despite the limitations of time to tell the story, there is no skewed interpretation and presentation regarding the portrayal of the reality. Two hundred actual 'Arnhem men' returned some, like Major Dickie Lonsdale and Major Freddie Gough, playing themselves. Others chosen were Irishmen Jack Bateman, John Daly and Tommy Scullion. Both Arnhem and Oosterbeek were as they were left after the battle, in ruins. In fact they were in even worse condition since on retaking the towns the Germans had indulged in a spate of looting.

In his 2002 book, *Brotherhood of the Cauldron: Irishmen in the 1st Airborne Division from North Africa to Arnhem*, David Truesdale, tells us:

When Hurst has to use shots of the fighting around Arnhem Bridge, the bridge had to be painted on to a sheet of glass to create the effect that it was still standing, when in fact it has been destroyed by air raids by the American Airforce on 6th and 7th October 1944. The film covers the actions around the bridge, the fighting in the suburbs of Oosterbeek and the eventual withdrawal across the Rhine. No blank ammunition was used; every shot fired and grenade thrown was real, as were the enemy tanks, although when the tanks are seen firing, a 'special effect' courtesy of Brocks, the fireworks manufacturers, was used, as was also the case with some of the shell bursts. Possibly it was felt that enough damage had been done to the locality. Practically all of the film was made in Holland.

The film opens with an overview of Arnhem in the aftermath of battle before a short documentary sequence outlining the basics of the plan. It then cuts to a barracks scene featuring ten paratroopers preparing for their last night in England before the operation. The voiceover names each of the soldiers, their pre-war occupation and place of origin; three of the ten were from Ireland. At the end of the film the scene returns to the barracks hut, and in a poignant ending two men, visibly older and subdued, enter in silence and sit amongst a row of empty beds with bedding folded upon them, possibly to represent that out of every ten who were involved in 'the Cauldron' only two returned. In the background, the 'Last Post' plays and the names of the ten paratroopers can be heard again. Over the top of this the voiceover says, 'Their manner of passing shall be carried like a banner borne high by all who should come after. Their story shall be told wherever men cherish deeds of good report. The story of those filthy, grimy, wonderful gentlemen who drop from the clouds and fight where they stand', before in the background can be heard 'Just ordinary men' as the film fades to black. Truesdale concludes: 'All in all, despite its age it remains one of the best accounts of the battle that has been committed to film.'

Born in Belfast, director Brian Desmond Hurst was probably Ireland's most prolific film director during the twentieth century. With over thirty films in various genres he had gone to Hollywood in the 1920s as an assistant to John Ford, returning to Britain in 1934 to begin his own career. Prior to 1945 he had worked on other war films, including *The Lion Has Wings* (1939), *Dangerous Moonlight* (1941) and *The Malta Story* (1953). During the war he made short propaganda films for the Ministry of Information such as *A Call For Arms* (1940), a rallying call for more women to work in the factories; *Miss Grant Goes to the Door* (1940), which prepared the nation for an invasion by Germany; and, *A Letter From Ulster* (1942), about the US Army training in Northern Ireland.

Hurst's lifelong friend and mentor, John Ford, was considered one of the greatest Hollywood directors. He won four Academy Awards as Best Director (he was a master of filming landscapes, many for Westerns), and one of his closest friends was Lord Killanin (Michael Morris). Both had involvement with D-Day and he later collaborated with Lord Killanin in the making of *The Quiet Man*. Born John Martin Aloysius Feeney in Portland, Maine, he was the eleventh and last child of Irish-speaking emigrants from Spiddal, County Galway.

Nowadays, the danger of Hollywood recreations of factual events is that of a new generation learning a version of the events that has been telescoped and made cinematic, unintentionally tampering with the authenticity, accuracy and message of what actually happened. This runs the risk of the development of myths, enhancements and the colouring of events for dramatic effect, thus contributing to the diminishing of the truth or a misrepresentation of the story. Despite its compression and omission of some events, and to today's cine-literate audience some 'hackneyed' dialogue, the sheer impact of a film like *Theirs is the Glory* is the film maker's decision to use the actual locations that featured in Operation Market Garden. To see the soldiers moving around the ruined streets of Oosterbeek, the Old Church or the ruined bridge at Arnhem, with 'bodies' scattered around portray at first hand the horrors that the Airborne Division had to endure.

Inherent to a book, a film, or a photograph is its narrative, and war has a narrative of its own. Depictions and descriptions of combat are by their nature at one remove from reality. The only thing like combat is combat itself, because it is contested, hostile, violent and horrible. Fortunately, as well as being good soldiers the Irish are good storytellers, and we can refer to books written by some who were at Arnhem or were otherwise closely involved with Operation Market Garden, for their perceptions of their participation. Monty's memoirs make reference to Arnhem in *The Memoirs of Field-Marshal the Viscount Montgomery of Alamein, KG* (1958), and Lieutenant Colonel 'Joe' Vandeleur in *A Soldier's Story* (1967). Lieutenant General Brian Horrocks described his experiences in two volumes, his autobiography *A Full Life* (1960) and in *Corps Commander* (1977), and Brigadier General John 'Shan' Hackett vividly described his wounding and being nursed back to health in *I Was a Stranger* (1978). Hackett, incidentally, went on to be both a successful author and soldier.

The telling of the Arnhem story and the brave part played by the individual Irish, whether officers or enlisted soldiers from all walks of life, demonstrates that courage is to be upheld as a source of national pride. As described by the narrator in *Theirs is The Glory*, 'They had fought a good fight and kept the faith … They stood against the enemy's armour and none had weakened. These knights of Arnhem had no armour, their strength was in their own courage and in each other … They have written in letters of fire an immortal page of history.'

EPILOGUE

Fighting for their Führer or their families, whether through misplaced loyalty or a misperception of mortal danger, the men of the Wehrmacht fought on furiously. This heroic but doomed German resistance had to be turned into a defeat by the Allies, a final crushing rout that would bring both German opposition and the war to an end. France was lost, the Allies were well lodged into the Low Countries (Belgium and Holland) and were now camped on Germany's doorstep. Hitler, however, was a long way from capitulating and he brought further misery and destruction to the German people. Hopeful of a disintegration in the Allied Coalition, he believed, 'The time will come when the tension between the Allies will become so great that the break will occur, and that the time for any favourable political dealings only comes when you are having military success.'

A delusional Hitler could not countenance that the time of Germany's military success was long over. He was fighting on two fronts and losing on both, his army all but defeated and his people utterly demoralised. Although Operation Market Garden had been unsuccessful, the Allies instead sought to clear the Scheldt Estuary of German resistance and bring Antwerp, a sea-going port already in Allied hands, into operation to directly address the problem of supplying the advance. This was achieved in late November 1944, and Hitler responded by unleashing V-1 and V-2 rocket strikes against Antwerp.

★★★

Epilogue

Not everyone who survived Arnhem was wounded, wound up as a prisoner of war or withdrew across the Lower Rhine. Of the 1st Airborne Division, there were those who escaped the notice of the German Army, hid and continued to evade capture. It became necessary for the Resistance to get these soldiers away from the Arnhem area, as their continued presence put their Dutch protectors in danger of German reprisals. Private Norman Dougan from County Armagh, 1st Parachute Regiment, was one such soldier. His brother, Robert 'Sandy' Dougan, also of the 1st Parachute Regiment, was among the first to die at Arnhem, killed in action on 17 September. Norman had been wounded in the thigh by a burst from an enemy machine-gun and was unable to make his way across the river during Operation Berlin (the evacuation across the Lower Rhine from the Oosterbeek perimeter during the night of 25–26 September). He was among those tasked to stay behind and make the Germans believe the Perimeter remained in place and continued to be defended. He was given a Sten gun and told to fire off his remaining ammunition until first light. With dawn breaking and all of his ammunition expended, instead of waiting for the Germans to realise they had been duped and patiently awaiting capture, he made his way into the woods and hid. Successfully evading German patrols, he made contact with the Dutch resistance and they arranged for him to remain hidden. A footnote in David Truesdale's book, *Brotherhood of the Cauldron*, describes the night of 22 October:

> Norman was one of 123 men to escape across the Rhine in Operation Pegasus (the successful evacuation of a large group of men who had been in hiding since the Battle of Arnhem). Led down to the riverbank through the darkness of a cold autumn night, Norman missed the rendezvous with the rescue boats and decided to swim across. It says something for his constitution that after nine days of combat, nearly a month hiding in various cellars and barns, and still with two bullets in his leg, he was able to cross a 300 yard wide swiftly flowing river in the darkness. Nevertheless, this is what he did.

Brigadier John 'Shan' Hackett, Commander of 4 Parachute Brigade, was another such escapee. Seriously wounded during the battle, his life was saved by a South-African surgeon, Alexander Lipmann-Kessel, who was serving as a captain in the Royal Army Medical Corps (RAMC). After a period of recuperation, he managed to escape from the hospital with the aid of the Resistance and was hidden by a Dutch family, the de Nooijs, in Ede. The family nursed Brigadier Hackett back to health over a period of several months and eventually he made a successful return to Allied lines.

Cork-born Major Mervyn Dennison, 3rd Parachute Battalion commanding A Company, was wounded in action at Arnhem, taken prisoner and sent to Spangenberg Castle, a moated fortress on top of a rock to the east of the German town of Kassel. He was a prisoner for six months, during which time he sat his Bar finals with the assistance of the Red Cross. He had just finished these when the Germans decided to move the prisoners west, away from the advancing Russians. As the column of men marched out of the castle, Dennison and one of his subalterns, Lieutenant Tony Baxter, slipped away while their comrades confused the guard dogs by blowing cigarette smoke in their faces. They managed to reach American lines and were soon repatriated to Britain, where Major Dennison ended the war serving with the Parachute Regiment in Dorset. Called to the Bar in Northern Ireland in 1945, he elected to join the Colonial Legal Service in 1947 and left to become a Crown Counsel in Northern Rhodesia. He was appointed a QC in 1960 and became a High Court Judge in Zambia in 1961. He returned to Northern Ireland in 1967 and worked as a clerk for Fermanagh County Council until 1973. He died in 1992, aged 78.

★★★

Nearly 500 Dutch citizens died during Operation Market Garden, many supporting the Allied troops fighting alongside the Americans or helping the British wounded. This anti-German sentiment and action did not go unpunished by the Germans, those in Arnhem were evicted from their homes, which were subsequently looted, and in the wider northern area of Holland still under German occupation the population was subjected to food shortages in reprisal. This atrocious situation was exacerbated by a freezing winter and scarcity of fuel. Such a severe combination of lack of food and deficit of fuel was made worse by sub-zero temperatures and nearly 20,000 people, many of them children, died before liberation brought relief in April 1945.

The aftermath of Operation Market Garden saw the theatre of operations swing from one salient – the large area of land controlled by the Allies – to another, the latter coming about by a shock German offensive. An attempted breakthrough by Panzer armies in the Ardennes, caused a 'bulge' in the line of the American First Army on 16 December. The Americans were caught unprepared for what became known as the Battle of the Bulge. A tangible connection between action in Arnhem and that in Ardennes was the use by German commandos of Jeeps captured at Arnhem in Operation Greif, a targeted attempt to sow confusion and mayhem in the American forces. German commandos of the 502nd SS Jägar Battalion, a Nazi commando-type Special Forces unit proficient in speaking English, wearing American uniforms, and driving American vehicles successfully infiltrated behind American lines. During December 1944, units of English-speaking German commandos misdirected US Army units and switched around road signs, sending troops in the wrong direction. As a result, US troops began asking other soldiers questions that they felt only Americans would know the answers to in order to flush out the German infiltrators, and the element of surprise having been lost the commandos abandoned the operation and reverted to wearing German uniforms.

There is an unusual Irish connection to the 502nd SS Jägar Battalion, since unlikely as it may seem, two members of the Battalion were Irishmen James Brady and Frank Stringer. They had joined the Royal Irish Fusiliers in 1938 and were posted together to Guernsey in the English Channel in 1940. One evening, having been denied service in a local pub, they became drunk and disorderly and received sentences of imprisonment which they were still serving when the Germans occupied Guernsey. They were handed over to the Wehrmacht by the Guernsey Police and became prisoners of war, initially at Camp Friesack in Brandenburg where they were put to work as farm labourers. The Abwehr, the German intelligence division, was fixated on the idea that Irishmen could be turned through Republican sympathies to working in Ireland against the British, and a small group of recruiters would tour the camps looking for people who would join up. Among the recruiters was Irish writer Francis Stuart, who had arrived in Germany in 1940 and was willing to work with the Abwehr. This led to Brady and Stringer taking up an offer of becoming members of the Waffen-SS as German soldiers and being given explosives training at the Abwehr training camp at Quentzgut. In 1944, they were recruited to the 502nd SS Jägar Battalion. Having participated in clandestine raids, operations and actions, even during the Battle of Berlin in 1945, Brady surrendered himself to the British. Brought to London, he was court-martialled and received a fifteen-year prison term, reduced when mitigation was brought to bear, he having been put into German hands by the Guernsey police. Back in Ireland in the 1950s, Stringer immigrated to Britain. Brady assumed his former real identity and both were slow, if ever, to mention their wartime experiences.

The Battalion was led by Austrian Lieutenant Colonel Otto Skorzeny, Hitler's favourite commando. He had previously been hand-picked by the Führer to lead a successful glider-borne rescue operation of Hitler's ally, Benito Mussolini, from an inaccessible and defended Italian mountain-top hotel, where he was being incarcerated having been overthrown. The Battalion were to cause later concerns when it was thought they had plans to assassinate General Eisenhower during Christmas week 1944 in Paris. This threat was taken so seriously that Eisenhower was temporarily confined to his Versailles headquarters. Had the attempt been carried through, it may also have resulted in causing casualties to those around him, one notable amongst them being Irishwoman Kay Summersby.

Kay McCarthy-Morrogh (her maiden name) spent a privileged and happy childhood in Inish Beg House, Baltimore, County Cork with a governess, post-hunt parties, sailing, horse riding and socialising. Her father had been a Lieutenant Colonel in the Royal Munster Fusiliers but was thoroughly 'black Irish', as she used to say of him. A noted beauty, she moved to London in her late teens and became among other involvements, a fashion model for *Worth*, the equivalent of being a supermodel today. There she married Gordon Thomas Summersby from whom she was later divorced but kept his surname. Subsequent to the outbreak of war, Kay joined the Mechanised Transport Corps and drove ambulances during the Blitz through the rubble-strewn streets in blackout conditions to horrific scenes of carnage, death and destruction, often ferrying bodies to morgues.

In May 1942, she was assigned as chauffeur to US General Eisenhower. A good driver, attractive, friendly, sociable and accomplished – in addition to possessing 'Irish' charm – a close wartime rapport was to develop between them, notwithstanding the enormous chasm in rank and an eighteen year age difference. On one occasion, journeying by sea to Tunisia to be with Eisenhower during Operation Torch, the troopship she was on, the *Strathallen*, was torpedoed and she had to abandon ship into the lifeboats. She was engaged to Major Richard 'Dick' Arnold, but he was killed whilst mine clearing in Tunisia in June 1943. Kay was to become Eisenhower's secretary and, breaking protocols, military etiquette and regulations, a closeness developed, their mutual attraction evident. Kay was almost always, but discretely, present.

That a strong relationship existed between them was never in doubt; that an actual affair ever occurred never clear-cut. The propriety or not of this relationship was never raised in circles, but certain assumptions were made and accepted. Kay accompanied General Eisenhower on 5 June 1944 as US Paratroopers boarded their aircraft prior to jumping out over Normandy before H-Hour on D-Day. She was also present and photographed in a US Army Group (later airbrushed out) at the formal surrender of the Germans. It was strongly speculated that Eisenhower sought counsel on the advisability of divorcing his wife Mamie to marry Kay, but was supposedly told in no uncertain terms that to do so would severely hamper any hopes of a future political career. Faced with the choice of life with Kay or a career in politics, Eisenhower chose the latter. He was subsequently to be twice elected US President in the 1950s. Kay was given American citizenship and made an officer in the Women's Army Corps (WAC) of the US Army, an unusual honour for a foreign national. Kay left the Army in 1947, having received a number of medals during her military career. She was to marry for a second time in 1952, to Reginald Heber Morgan, a stockbroker, but this marriage too ended in divorce six years later. Kay Summersby died of cancer at her home in Southampton, Long Island in January 1975 at the age of 65. Her ashes were brought back to West Cork by her brother Seamus (himself a British Commando during the war) and scattered over the family grave.

As for her would-be assassin, Otto Skorzeny was to cause much intrigue. He arrived to Ireland in 1959 and purchased Martinstown House and farm in County Kildare near the Curragh. His journey there began at the war's end, ten days after Hitler committed suicide in May 1945, when Skorzeny surrendered to the Americans. He was to stand trial for war crimes in Dachau in 1947, but the case collapsed and he was acquitted. Still to face charges from other countries, he was detained but escaped. He went to Madrid and established an import/export agency, which was suspected of being a front organisation assisting the escape of wanted Nazis from Europe to South America. He was to make many trips to Argentina, meeting President Juan Perón and becoming a bodyguard to Perón's wife, Eva. Skorzeny supposedly stopped an attempt on her life and was rumoured to have had an affair with her.

Six foot four inches in height and weighing eighteen stone (114 kg), Skorzeny had a distinctive scar running along his left cheek, a reminder of a duelling encounter from his student days. Arriving to Ireland for a visit in June 1957, he was to return two years later and take up residence on the Curragh. There were reported allegations that he had opened up an escape route for ex-Nazis in Spain and that his County Kildare farm was a holding facility, sheltering them, but this claim was unsubstantiated. A further layer of intrigue lingers around Otto Skorzeny, as there were suggestions that he was later 'turned' by Israel's intelligence service, the Mossad, and was working for them helping to track ex-Nazis. He was not granted permanency of residence in Ireland and returned to Madrid, where he died of cancer in 1975.

★★★

Epilogue

Montgomery, in his 1958 memoir, gave four reasons for not gaining 'complete success at Arnhem': First, he says, the Operation was not regarded at Supreme Headquarters as the spearhead of a major Allied movement on the northern flank (neither prioritised nor resourced accordingly); second, the Airborne forces at Arnhem were dropped too far away from their vital objective and it was some hours before they reached it, thus giving the Germans time to rally; third, the weather; and fourth because the 2nd SS Panzer Corps was refitting in the Arnhem area having limped there after its mauling in Normandy. 'We knew it was there but we were wrong in supposing that it could not fight effectively; its battle state was far beyond our expectation.' He concluded his chapter on Arnhem with the following paragraph:

> In my prejudiced view, if the operation had been properly backed from its inception and given the aircraft, ground forces, and administrative (logistic) resources necessary for the job, it would have succeeded in spite of my mistakes, or the adverse weather, or the presence of the 2nd SS Panzer Corps in the Arnhem area. I remain Market Garden's unrepentant advocate.

Despite not having succeeded at Arnhem, Monty's imaginative concept for the strategic use of airborne forces did not deter the Allies from using them tactically later on. The deployment for Operation Varsity (24 March 1945) saw the 6th British and 17th US Airborne Divisions dropped beyond the River Rhine to help develop Operation Plunder's bridgehead across the river and increase the feasibility of a rapid breakout. Approximately 22,000 (21,680) paratroopers and glider-borne troops were transported in over 1,500 (1,696) aircraft and 1,300 (1,348) gliders, with nearly 900 fighters escorting them, to form an immense air armada. Inserted in one lift in just over an hour, neither too far ahead of ground troops nor too far away from their objectives, their arrival had a disadvantageous psychological impact on the German defenders and created the conditions in which major objectives were taken. Falling within the familiar remit of their tasking: the seizure of key ground objectives and bridges, securing the area to prevent against German counter attack, and linking up with the advancing ground forces (Operation Plunder), it was similar to those undertaken in Operation Overlord pre H-Hour on D-Day. In the event, they succeeded in protecting the developing ground-force lodgement on the east bank of the Rhine and provided the means for a breakout to win the war.

Freedom from fascism – Hitler's political system of extreme right-wing dictatorship – the liberation of Europe and making the world safe for democracy again was what was at stake, and to do so the world went to war for the second time in the twentieth century. There was much death and destruction, but peace and freedom have a price and the world paid it. There is an important lesson here to not to take democracy for granted in our daily lives. That and there is no room for hate, because when you hate something you become a captive to it.

BIBLIOGRAPHY

Badsey, Stephen, *Arnhem 1944* (Oxford: Osprey Publishing Ltd, 1993).

Beevor, Antony, *Arnhem: The Battle for the Bridges, 1944* (New York: Viking Press, 2018).

Clark, Lloyd, *Crossing the Rhine: Breaking into Nazi Germany 1944–1945* (New York: Atlantic Monthly Press, 2008).

Farrington, Karen, *Normandy to Berlin: Into the Heart of the Third Reich* (London: Arcturus Publishing, 2005).

Forty, Simon and Timmermans, Tom, *Operation Market Garden: September 1944* (Havertown, PA: Casemate Publishers, 2018).

Harclerode, Peter, *Arnhem: A Tragedy of Errors* (London: Caxton Publishers, 1994).

Harvey, Arnold D., *Arnhem* (London: Cassell & Co., 2001).

Montgomery, Bernard Law, *The Memoirs of Field-Marshal the Viscount Montgomery of Alamein, K.G.* (London: Collins, 1958).

Piekalkiewicz, Janusz, *Arnhem 1944* (Shepperton: Ian Allan Publishers Ltd., 1977).

Ryan, Cornelius, *A Bridge Too Far* (London: Hamish Hamilton, 1974).

Smyth, Jack, *Five Days in Hell* (London: William Kimber & Co., 1956).

Truesdale, David, *Brotherhood of the Cauldron: Irishmen in the 1st Airborne Division from North Africa to Arnhem* (Newtownards: Redcoat Publishing, 2002).

GLOSSARY

Army	Two or more Corps acting together under the overall command of a General.
Army Group	Two or more armies acting under the command of a Field Marshal.
Bailey Bridge	A temporary structure that can be erected in hours to span a river and is strong enough to support the weight of a tank. Of British design, the bridge is broken into parts and can be carried on transport vehicles.
Battalion	An infantry unit of 500–800 soldiers commanded by a Lieutenant Colonel.
Brigade	Two or more Battalions under the overall command of a Brigadier.
Brigade Group	A Brigade with attached support units; e.g. medical staff, engineers, and anti-tank gunners.
C-47 Dakota	A transport aircraft used by the Allies for dropping paratroopers or supplies. Of US design, in Operation Market Garden the C-47 was used to tow gliders to the Landing Zones.
CG-4A Waco	The standard glider of the US Army, it was named 'Hadrian' by the British Army. Constructed of fabric-covered wood and metal, the Waco was cheap and easy to mass produce. However, it was not as robust as the British Horsa and was prone to structural failure.
Company	A sub-division of a Battalion, commanded by a Major

	and consisting of approximately 120 men.
Corps	Two or more Divisions acting together under the overall command of a Lieutenant General.
Division	Two or more Brigades and assorted supporting units (e.g. artillery, engineers) acting together under the command of a Major General. Typically, a Division would consist of 10,000 personnel.
Drop Zone	An area of land designated for the dropping of paratroopers.
DUKW	A US designed 2.5 ton amphibious vehicle used by the Allies to transport goods and troops over land and water.
Hamilcar	The largest of the British gliders, designed to carry heavy equipment (e.g. 17-pound anti-tank guns, Bren carriers, or light tanks).
Horsa	The standard British glider. Built of wood and capable of carrying twenty-six men, or heavy equipment such as Jeeps and 6-pound anti-tank guns.
Landing Zone	An area designated for the landing of gliders.
Lee–Enfield No. 4	The standard British infantry rifle, it was adopted for standard use in 1941.
PIAT	Projector, Infantry Anti-Tank. A British-made hand-held anti-tank weapon that fires a 2.5 pound (1.1 kg) shaped charge. Best for dealing with lightly armoured vehicles, it was a 'line of sight' weapon that often left the user exposed to fire from the enemy.
Platoon	Consisting of up to sixty soldiers commanded by a Lieutenant. Glider-borne units consisted of twenty-six men so that they could be transported in a single Horsa glider.
Salient	Also known as a bulge, a Salient is where the front line between two opposing forces projects into one force's territory. The salient is surrounded by the enemy on multiple sides, making the troops occupying the area

	vulnerable to being 'pinched' across the base and becoming isolated.
Sapper	A private soldier in the Royal Engineers. Sappers are responsible for tasks such as building and repairing roads and bridges, laying and clearing mines, etc.
Self-propelled gun	A large artillery gun mounted on its own motorised vehicle. Unlike static artillery guns that are towed behind Jeeps, self-propelled guns are more flexible in use.
Slit trench	A one-man trench dug by infantry for protection in firefights and against artillery bombardment.
Schutzstaffel (SS)	Literally translated as 'Protection Squad', the SS were separate to the Wehrmacht and were under the overall control of Himmler. The Waffen-SS were the military wing of the Nazi Party.
Sten gun	A light machine-gun usually carried by British officers and NCO's.
USAAF	United States Army Air Force. Unlike the RAF, the US air forces during the war were not an independent service, but instead fell under the jurisdiction of either the navy or the army.
Wehrmacht	The armed forces of Nazi Germany from 1935 to 1945, it consisted of the Heer (the regular German Army), the Kriegsmarine (the Navy) and the Luftwaffe (air force). It did not include the SS.

ABBREVIATIONS

AA	Anti-Aircraft (Ack Ack)
AWOL	Absent Without Leave
BEF	British Expeditionary Force
CB	Counter Battery Fire
CCS	Casualty Clearing Station
DSO	Distinguished Service Order
DZ	Drop Zone
FAAA	First Allied Airborne Army
FEBA	Forward Edge of the Battle Area
FOO	Forward Observation Officer
KIA	Killed in Action
LZ	Landing Zone
MFC	Mortar Fire Controller
MC	Military Cross
POW	Prisoner of War
RAF	Royal Air Force
RAMC	Royal Army Medical Corps
SAS	Special Air Service
SHAEF	Supreme Headquarters Allied Expeditionary Force
SOE	Special Operations Executive
VC	Victoria Cross
WIA	Wounded in Action
XXX Corps	30th Corps

CHRONOLOGY

June–September 1944

The rapid advance in northern Europe after D-Day results in supply and fuel resupply difficulties being experienced by the Allies.

2 September 1944

Operation Comet, a limited airborne using the British 1st Airborne Division, along with the Polish 1st Independent Parachute Brigade, to secure several bridges over the Rhine River to aid the Allied advance into Germany is cancelled after several days of bad weather and concerns over increasing levels of German resistance.

10 September 1944

In a meeting with General Eisenhower, Montgomery proposes a more ambitious Allied plan to cross the Rhine with large forces and open a route for an Allied advance towards Germany and Berlin.

11 September

Eisenhower gives the go ahead for the operation, a combined air assault – the 'Market' phase using the airborne forces of Lieutenant General Lewis H. Brereton's First Allied Airborne Army to seize bridges and other terrain – and 'Garden', using ground forces of the Second Army to move north spearheaded by XXX Corps under Lieutenant-General Brian Horrocks.

17 September	Operation Market Garden commences on a positive note with Allied success all round. The British 1st Airborne Division is dropped near Arnhem and Oosterbeek, the US 82nd Airborne Division near Nijmegen and Grave, and the US 101st Airborne Division near Son and Voghel. The US 82nd Airborne Divisions are successful in capturing their target bridges. In the south, the 101st capture four of the five bridges assigned to them. British paratroopers landing at Arnhem encounter the 9th and 10th SS Panzer Divisions, who are in the area undergoing maintenance. The northern end of the bridge at Arnhem is captured but the British force is quickly cut off from help by the Germans. At the 'start line' Lieutenant General Brian Horrocks gives the order to advance, but the Irish Guards meet heavy resistance and only get as far as Valkenswaard.
18 September 1944	The Second Airborne Lift gets underway after a delay due to fog. Reinforcements arrive at the Drop Zones and near Arnhem British paratroopers advance to reinforce the troops holding the bridge but are held up by heavy German resistance. The Germans blow up the bridge at Son, halting the advance of XXX Corps and mount counter-attacks against the British holding the bridge at Arnhem, suffering heavy losses.
19 September 1944	The 1 Parachute Brigade begins an attack to relieve the British at the bridge at Arnhem but are spotted and halted by fire from the main German defensive line in open ground. The

British suffer heavy losses and retreat towards Oosterbeek. There the British withdraw into a defensive perimeter and hold a bridgehead on the north bank of the Rhine, while at the Arnhem bridge the British continue to hold on to their positions. The Allied forces are supported by the Third Airborne Lift, a portion of the Polish 1st Independent Parachute Brigade and its anti-tank battery. Deployed into a Landing Zone controlled by the Germans, they suffer heavy losses but arrive south of the river into Driel. After a 12-hour delay the Bailey bridge at Son is completed and XXX Corps advance to reach Nijmegen.

20 September 1944   At the bridge at Arnhem, Lieutenant Colonel John Frost's force continue to hold but are running low on ammunition, especially anti-tank munitions. A two-hour truce is agreed to evacuate the wounded (including Lieutenant Colonel Frost) into German captivity. Major Freddie Gough takes over as commander and leads a remnant of the group in withdrawal from the bridge toward Oosterbeek, not knowing that the troops there were preparing for their last stand. The British at Oosterbeek are formed into a defensive perimeter and begin their final resistance. In Nijmegen the US 82nd Airborne capture the bridge and XXX Corps comes under attack from German forces on the Groesbeek Heights, but drives them back.

21 September 1944   The 1st Airborne Division establish a perimeter in the buildings and woods around Oosterbeek

with the intention of holding a bridgehead on the north side of the Rhine until XXX Corps arrive. The perimeter forces fight off several German assaults, including one heavy attack repulsed by the 'Lonsdale Force'. After two days delay, the remainder of the Polish 1st Independent Parachute Brigade under Major-General Stanisław Sosabowski are dropped opposite the 1st Airborne Division's position south of the Rhine near Driel. Meanwhile, XXX Corps are still held at Nijmegen while in Arnhem, the remaining paratroopers at the bridge surrender to the German Army.

22 September 1944   The 43rd Infantry advances from Nijmegen but only gets as far as Elst while the Germans attack the 'Corridor' (nicknamed 'Hell's Highway') and force XXX Corps to send troops back to Veghel to support the 101st Airborne. In Oosterbeek, the Germans bombard the 1st Airborne positions mercilessly causing heavy casualties on a day that becomes known as 'Black Friday'. The presence of the Polish 1st Independent Parachute Brigade confuses the Germans into thinking that this is another advance on Arnhem and redeploy troops from Oosterbeek, giving some respite to the 1st Airborne but having little effect on the Polish force.

23 September 1944   The weather improves and the Fifth Airborne Lift is able to drop reinforcements near Overasselt and Son. The Corridor is reopened by XXX Corps and the British occupy Elst. In Oosterbeek, the Germans continue to

bombard the 1st Airborne and attempt to cut the British off from the river bank. They fail and the Polish 1st Independent Parachute Brigade manage to reinforce the perimeter with some 200 troops.

24 September 1944 — The principal objective of Operation Market Garden, the Allied crossing of the Rhine, is abandoned and the decision made to set up a new defensive line in Nijmegen. The Allies attempt to reinforce the perimeter at Oosterbeek with the 4th Battalion, The Dorsetshire Regiment, but the Dorsets land amongst German positions. Suffering heavy losses, it is decided to withdraw the 1st Airborne Division from the perimeter.

25–26 September 1944 — The 1st Airborne Division receive orders to withdraw across the Rhine, but the effort, known as Operation Berlin, cannot proceed until nightfall. During the day the perimeter comes under heavy and sustained attack and the resistance nearly collapses. The 1st Airborne Division holds out and under cover of darkness the 2,400 surviving troops are evacuated to the southern bank. To allow the 1st Airborne to escape, wounded troops are given weapons and what ammunition remains to fool the Germans into thinking the perimeter is still putting up a viable resistance. Operation Berlin marks the end of the Battle of Arnhem.

October 1944 — The defensive line continued to be held by Allied positions in the Nijmegen Salient, as it came to be known, and were manned by airborne units. On 2 October 1944, the shipping route to Antwerp was opened up by Canadian, British and Polish forces in the Battle of the Scheldt, which concluded after five weeks of hard fighting and over 12,000 Allied casualties.

22–23 October 1944   Following Operation Market Garden and the evacuation of the 1st Airborne in Oosterbeek, approximately 500 Allied troops were still hiding from the German Army, including some who had escaped from the perimeter. Operation Pegasus was organised in conjunction with the Dutch resistance to evacuate as many of these troops as possible. Overnight, approximately 150 men were ferried across the Rhine and later flown back to England to re-join the troops who were evacuated during Operation Berlin.

February–March 1945   After a delay in the deployment of forces because of the Battle of the Bulge, the last German offensive of the Second World War, Operation Veritable was an Allied offensive to clear German forces from the area between the Rhine and Maas rivers, east of the German/ Dutch frontier, in the Rhineland.

23–27 March 1945   On the night of 23 March 1945, the 21st Army Group under Field Marshal Bernard Montgomery crossed the Rhine at Rees, Wesel, and south of the river Lippe by the British Second Army, under Lieutenant General Sir Miles Dempsey, and the United States Ninth Army, under Lieutenant General William H. Simpson. Alongside the ground invasion, known as Operation Plunder, an airborne invasion, Operation Varsity, dropped more than 16,000 paratroopers from several thousand aircraft. It was the largest airborne operation in history to be conducted on a single day and in one location. Lessons were learned from Operation Market Garden in that the paratroopers were dropped close to their objectives and with adequate support.

12–16 April 1945   From the front established around Nijmegen, three Canadian infantry brigades of the 49th Division entered Arnhem from the east and within four days the city was finally under Allied control. The liberation of Arnhem was bittersweet, after recapturing the city from the British after Operation Market Garden, the German Army had evicted all of the Dutch living there and systematically looted the city, leaving behind buildings that were little more than empty shells. Two weeks after the battle a general truce brought major combat operations in Holland to an end, and on 5 May the German Commander in Chief surrendered to the Canadian Army. Three days later Germany unconditionally surrendered, bringing the war in Europe to a close.

INDEX

Abwehr, the, 114
Adair, Maj Gen Allan, 3
aircraft, 22, 117–18; B-26 Marauder
 bomber (US), 80; C-47 Dakota
 transport plane (US), vii, viii, ix, 18,
 29, 50, 66, 80–2; Hamilcar glider (UK),
 25, 67; Hawker Typhoon fighter-
 bomber (UK), 23, 31, 66; Horsa glider
 (UK), 25, 79, 80
Allied strategy, 11–14, 26–8, 43–4, 49–50,
 54–5, 58–9, 62, 77–8, 89, 95–8, 101–2,
 117–18; and the air drops and the
 element of surprise, 1, 3, 7–10, 14–16,
 34–5, 36, 41
ambitions and rivalries, 19–20
Arnold, Maj Richard 'Dick,' 115
Attenborough, Richard, 105

Barry, Lt Peter, 36–7
Bateman, Jack, 106
battery and mortar fire, the, 74, 91
Battle of Arnhem, the, 33, 36–58, 75
Battle of El Alamein, the, 6
Battle of Normandy, the, 7, 9–10, 11, 14
Battle of the Bulge, the, 91, 113
Baxter, Lt Tony, 112
BEF (British Expeditionary Force), the, 6

Belcher, Pte First Class, 25
Bermingham, Sgt John, 51
Bittrich, Obergruppenfuhrer Wilhelm, 34,
 65–6, 76
Blake, Maj Tony, 69–70, 74
Blatch, Maj John, 81
Blitzkrieg, 2
bocage countryside of Normandy, 7, 8, 14
books and films, 105–9
Boyd, Sgt James Frederick 'Paddy,' 29, 30,
 82
Brackstone, Sgt Charles Thomas, 25
Brady, James, 113–14
Breen, Lance Cpl Tom 'Paddy,' 100
Brereton, Lt Gen Lewis Hyde, 1, 15–16,
 96
Brett, Capt Peter, 104
Bridge Too Far, A (book & film), 103–4,
 105–6
Briody, Sgt Maj Michael, 43, 79–80
British Army, the: 1st Airborne Div, viii,
 1, 2, 4, 12, 13, 16, 31, 32, 41, 54–5,
 66, 72, 77, 84, 88, 94–5, 102; 1st
 Parachute Bde, 36, 51, 111; 1st Bn,
 38, 42, 44, 51, 57–8, 59, 88; 2nd Bn,
 37–8, 39, 41–2, 46, 50, 61, 88, 97;
 3rd Bn, 37, 38, 40, 42, 44, 45, 46,

57–8, 59, 112; 4th Parachute Bde, 30, 42, 46, 51–2, 56–7, 58, 88; 10th Bn, 43, 57, 58, 71, 72, 83; 11th Bn, 43, 46, 57–8, 59; 156th Bn, 30, 43, 57, 59, 88, 98; 1st Special Air Service Brigade, 1; 2nd Army, 13; Guards Armoured Div, 3, 27, 62, 82, 90; VIII Corps, 13, 95; XII Corps, 13, 95; XXX Corps, 3, 4, 10, 13, 19, 26, 31, 47, 48, 53, 54, 55, 62, 66, 70, 72, 88, 95, 98, 100; 6th Airborne Div, 2; 21st Independent Parachute Company, 22, 32, 42, 59, 71, 83; Airlanding Bde, 69; Border Rgt 1st Bn, 42, 75; KOSB 7th Bn, 42, 59, 75, 83; South Staffordshire 2nd Bn, 42, 46, 57–8, 59, 64; Dorsetshire Regiment: 4th Bn, 97–8; Glider Parachute Rgt, 43; Irish Guards, 3, 9, 92; 2nd Bn, 93; Mobile Reconnaissance Squadron, 33, 39; Polish 1st Independent Parachute Bde, 12, 16, 34, 52, 58, 59, 66–7, 97; Reconnaisance Company, 35; Royal Armoured Corps, 28; Royal Army Medical Corps, 30, 72, 83, 112; Royal Army Service Corps, 4, 50, 79; Royal Engineers Corps, 28, 100
Brotherhood of the Cauldron: Irishmen in the 1st Airborne Division from North Africa to Arnhem (book), 106–7, 111
Browning, Lt Gen Frederick Arthur Montague 'Boy,' 1, 16–17, 19, 34, 35, 48, 60–1, 84, 96, 97, 105
Buchanan, Lt 'Bucky,' 99
Buchanan, Rev Capt Alan Alexander, 99
Byman, Guy, 104

Cain, Maj Robert, 64, 65
Call for Arms, A (film), 108
Cameron, Pte James, 22
Capa, Robert, 106
capture of Operation Market Garden plans, 43, 49
Cassidy, Lt Col Patrick, 23–4, 31, 53–4
casualties, 19, 28, 30, 31, 32, 50–1, 52, 57, 60, 61, 67, 72, 80, 82–3, 98, 102, 112
CB (Counter-battery) fire, 74
chaplaincies and spiritual aid, 99
Chill, Generalleutnant Kurt, 33, 89
Churchill, Winston, 2, 9, 96
Cockings, Sgt E.G.J., 22
communications, 41, 48, 53, 70, 79
Conway, Lance Cpl J.J., 30
Conway, Pte E.M., 29–30
Cooney, Gunner M., 42
Cooney, Pte W. 'Paddy,' 97
Corps Commander (book), 109
Cox, Lance Cpl Mick, 29, 30, 39, 48, 62
Crittenden, Lt Bob, 80

D-Day landings, the (*see* Operation Overlord (June 1944))
Daly, Sgt John Joseph, 42, 64–5
defensive trenches, 75, 77
Dempsey, Gen Sir Miles C., 13
Dennison, Maj Mervyn, 37, 40, 45–6, 112
Devlin, Capt Brian, 83
Devlin, Pte William Patrick, 60
Diffin, Pte Norman, 29, 30
Dobie, Lt Col David, 36
Dolaghan, Pte Francis, 30, 52
Dolaghan, Pte Thomas, 30, 52
Doran, Gunner Joseph, 42
Dorman, Lt A.E., 93, 94
Dougan, Pte Norman, 111

Index

Dougan, Pte Robert 'Sandy,' 30, 111
du Maurier, Daphne, 19
Dunbar, Lance Cpl Thomas, 22, 82
Dutch civilian support, 112–13
Dutch underground (PAN), the, 99–100, 105, 111

Earls, Pte Richard, 83
Eccles, D.L., 98
Egan, Fr Bernard, 38, 99
Eisenhower, Gen Dwight D., 7, 8, 9, 11, 12, 13, 14, 19, 96, 114, 115
element of surprise, the, 35, 36, 39; in Allied airborne drops, 1, 3, 7–10, 14–16, 34–5, 41
Enigma code, the, 20
ex-Nazis after the war, 116

FEBA (Forward Edge of the Battle Area), 13
Feehily, Sgt Brian Patrick Sheridan, 43
Fiely, Pte James, 22, 71, 72
Finn, Pte James 'Jimmy,' 83
Finucane, 'Paddy,' 19
'Firefly' Sherman tank (US), 31, 53, 94
First Allied Airborne Army, the, 1, 13, 15, 19, 28, 33, 43, 96
First World War, the, 2
Fitch, Lt Col John, 36, 42
Five Days in Hell (book), 105
'Flak Alley,' 22
Flanagan, Trooper James, 90–2
Flynn, Pte James 'Paddy,' 83
FOO (Forward Observation Officer), 74
Ford, John, 108
Frost, Lt Col John Dutton, 36, 37, 41, 46, 61, 85, 99
Fryer, Lance Sgt John 'Jack,' 88
Full Life, A (book), 109

Gavin, Lt Gen James 'Jumpin' Jim,' 24, 32, 53
Gavin, Martin and Mary, 2
German Army, the, 8; 9th SS Aufklärung-Abteilung (reconnaissance battalion), 46; 9th SS Panzer Div, 76; 10th SS Panzer Corps, 61; 502nd SS Jägar Bn, 113, 114; 506th Heavy Tank Bn, 89; Fallschirmjäger paratroopers, 2; II SS Panzer Corps, 76, 117; Kampfgruppe Chill, 89; Kampfgruppe Huber, 76; Kampfgruppe Krafft, 75; Kampfgruppe Walther, 26, 76; Knast Kampfgruppe, 47
German military strategy, 2, 4, 19, 26, 65–6, 84; and defence tactics, 27, 31, 32, 33–4, 35–6, 37, 38, 41, 46–7, 110
Gerraghty, Pte Tom (McCluskey), 88
Gestapo, the, 104
glider crashes, 32, 80
Gorman, Lt John, 93–4
Gough, Maj Freddie, 33, 36, 39, 61, 106
Gräbner, SS-Hauptsturmführer Viktor, 47
Grace, Lance Cpl James, 50–1

Hackett, Brig Gen John 'Shan,' 43, 46, 47, 51–2, 56, 57, 59, 86–8, 109, 112
Hamilton, Gunner Thomas, 42
Harbinson, Lance Sgt, 93
Harrington, Lance Cpl Patrick, 60
Harzer, Obersturmbannführer Walter, 76
Heathcoat-Amory, Lt Col Derick, 87
Heathcote, Lt Keith, 26
Hicks, Brig Philip 'Pip,' 42, 46, 59
Hitler, Adolf, 19, 27, 33, 110, 114
Horrocks, Lt Gen Brian, 3, 19, 26, 31, 76, 88, 89, 109
Houston, Maj James Ivor 'Happy,' 60

Index

Hunter, Sgt John, 60
Hurley, Pte Patrick, 72
Hurst, Brian Desmond, 106, 107–8

I Was a Stranger (book), 109
Irish Defence Forces, the, 83

'Joe's Bridge' (De Groote Barrier bridge,
    capture of, 9–10

Kaminski, Janusz, 106
Kampfgruppen (battle groups), 26, 33 (*see also*
    German Army, the)
Kavanagh, Capt Desmond, 49, 50
Kendrick, Pte Samuel John, 29, 88
Kilmartin, Lt Michael, 51
King, Flt Lt Harry, ix

Lathbury, Brig Gen Gerald, 42, 46
Lee, Sgt Lawrence, 29, 30
Letter from Ulster, A (film), 108
Lipmann-Kessel, Alexander 'Lippy,' 88, 112
Lonsdale, Maj Richard 'Dickie,' 59, 60,
    106
'Lonsdale Force,' the, 59, 60
Lord, Lt David 'Lummy,' vii–ix, 50
Lynas, Lance Cpl Ernest, 98

Mackay, Capt Eric, 47
Mackenzie, Lt Col Charles, 97
Maltby, Lt Ralph Alexander, 23, 43
Masterson, Sgt Eric George Wolf, 43
Matson, Sgt Eric, 67, 97
Maxted, Stanley, 104
McCormick, Pte Frank, 88
McCrory, Sgt James 'Paddy,' 53–4
McKinley, Flying Off Henry, 80, 81–2
medical aid, 72, 83, 88, 90, 91, 99, 112

*Memoirs of Field-Marshal the Viscount
    Montgomery of Alamein, KG, The*
    (book), 109, 117
military doctrine, 14, 44, 56, 62, 64, 70–1
military honours, 10, 24, 46, 47, 59, 61,
    65, 70, 79, 81–2, 83, 92, 93
Millar, Lt G.R. 'Dusty,' 43
Miss Grant Goes to the Door (film), 108
'Moaning Minnie' rocket launcher
    (Germany), 37, 69
Model, Generalfeldmarschall Walter, 33–4
Montgomery, Field Marshal Bernard Law,
    3, 5, 6–9, 10, 11–12, 13–14, 101, 103,
    105; and ambitions to control Allied
    strategy, 19, 96; memoirs of, 109, 117
Moore, Rev J.C., 3
Morgan, Reginald Heber, 116
Morris, Michael (Lord Killanin), 108
mortar bombs, 73–5, 76, 91
Mossad, the, 116
Murphy, Sgt Andrew, 67
Murray, Lt Col Ian, 88
Mussolini, Benito, 114
Myers, Lt Col Eddie, 97

Nally, James, 24
Neville, Lance Cpl Daniel, 38, 47, 61
Newell, Pte Cecil, 38
Nijmegen bridge, 32, 47, 53, 61–2, 94

O'Connor, Gen Richard, 13
Oflag XII-A POW camp, 30
O'Hagan, Pte Patrick, 24–5
Oliver, Maj Roy, 104
O'Neal, Staff Sgt Russell, 21
Oosterbeek perimeter and bridge, Arnhem,
    37–9, 41, 58, 60, 63–5, 69–72, 82–9,
    94–5, 111

Operation Berlin (September 1944), 98, 100–1, 111

Operation Comet, 11–12

Operation Dynamo (June 1940), 6

Operation Market Garden (Sept 1944), viii–ix, 1–2, 3–6, 10, 13, 21–3, 26–8, 32–3, 101–2, 117; evacuation across the lower Rhine, 98, 100–1, 111; 'Garden' push to Eindhoven, 26–9, 31–2; idea of, 12–13; planning of, 10–17, 20, 21

Operation Overlord (June 1944), vii–viii, 7–8, 14

Operation Pegasus, 30

Operation Varsity (March 1945), 117

operational drops, 21–2, 23–5, 32, 34, 35, 42, 52, 97

PAN (Dutch undeground), the, 99–100, 105, 111

paratroop jumps (*see* operational drops)

Parker, Sgt D.S., 43

Pathfinder paratroopers, 22, 32

Patton, Gen George S., 8, 11, 13

'perimeter defence' lines, 70–1

Perón, Eva, 116

Perón, Juan, 116

physical and psychological impacts, 20–2, 31, 54, 67–8, 77, 86, 98–9

Place, Lt Col John W., 23, 43

POWs, 30, 31, 65, 99, 112, 113–14

Queen Alexandra Nursing Corps, 28

Quiet Man, The (film), 108

Quinn, Sgt Peter, 100–1

RAF, the, 2, 22, 31, 72, 88; 271 Sqn, vii, 50

recreations of factual events, 108–9

recruitment in Ireland, 29

regimental composition of Irish officers, 28–9

Reinhard, Generalleutnant Hans, 33

Reuters News Agency, 103, 104

risk evaluation and military planning, 14–15, 20

Ritchie, Gen Neil, 13

Rundstedt, Generalfeldmarschall Gerd von, 34

Russell, Lt I.A., 38

Ryan, Cornelius, 103–4

Ryan, Katherine, 24

SAS (Special Air Service), the, 1, 2

Saunders, Pte William, 38

Saving Private Ryan (film), 106

Scullion, Pte Tommy, 71, 106

Shanahan, Rifleman John, 90

Siggins, Lt Donald, 42

Simpson, Sgt Thomas John Duncan, 43

Sint-Oedenrode fighting, 90–1

Skorzeny, Lt Col Otto, 114, 116

Smith, Warrant Off Albert, 80–1

Smyth, Jack, 103, 104–5

SOE (Special Operations Executive), the, 2

Soldier's Story, A (book), 109

Sosabowski, Maj Gen Stanislaw, 34, 66, 89, 96, 98

Spielberg, Steven, 106

Stalag 11-B POW camp, 30

Stalag XI-B POW camp, 65, 99

Stringer, Frank, 113–14

Stuart, Francis, 114

Student, Gen Kurt, 2, 35, 76

Stug assault gun (Germany), 45

Sullivan, Pte Patrick, 67

Summersby, Gordon Thomas, 115

Index

Summersby, Kay (née McCarthy-Morrogh), 114–16
supply dropping zones, 49, 50
supply logistics, 8, 9, 12, 13, 35, 49, 50–1, 52–3, 54, 62, 72–3, 78–9, 82, 88, 89
Swiecicki, Marek, 104

Taylor, Maj Gen Maxwell, 23, 31
Tettau, Generalleutnant Hans von, 76
Theirs is the Glory: Men of Arnhem (film), 106, 108
Thomas, Maj Gen Ivor, 89
Thompson, Lt Col W.F.K. 'Sheriff,' 59–60
Tiger heavy tank (Germany), 64–5, 78, 89, 94
time and space in military planning, 7, 10
Tottenham, Capt Charles Barton, 92–3
Towhy, Pte John, 32
training, 44, 77, 79, 104, 108, 114
Truesdale, David, 106–7, 111

urban warfare, 44–5, 48
Urquhart, Maj Gen Robert Elliot 'Roy,' 42, 46, 54, 58, 84, 85, 96, 97, 100
US Army, the, 1; 82nd Airborne Div, 1, 2, 3, 16, 21, 24, 47, 53, 61–2, 82, 89; 101st Airborne Div, 1, 2, 3, 16, 18, 31–2, 82, 89; 501st Airborne Rgt, 23;

501st PIR, 32; 502nd PIR, 32, 53, 90; 506th PIR, 32; First Army, 113; WAC (Women's Army Corps), 115–16
USAAF, the, viii, 2

V-2 missile attacks, 12, 96, 110
Vandeleur, Lt Col John Ormsby Evelyn 'Joe,' 3, 9–10, 26, 109
Vickers K-type machine gun (UK), 61
Vint, Gunner F.W., 42

Walther, Col Erich, 26
war correspondents, 103–5
War Diary of the Irish Guards, The (book), 93–4
War of Independence, the, 6
weaponry: Bren light machine-gun (UK), 64; M1 Garand rifle (US), 24, 91; MG 42 machine gun (Germany), 91; PIAT anti-tank weapon (UK), 63–4, 65, 78
Wetheral, Sgt J.A.B., 43
Williams, Flt Lt Billy, 104
Williams, Gunner E., 42
Williams, Maj Gen Paul L., 43, 96
Wilson, Pte Thomas, 88
Wood, Alan, 104
Woods, Lt Reginald Bryan 'Danny Boy,' 37–8, 52, 65